EASY
Indonesian

Katherine Davidsen has lived and worked in Jakarta, Indonesia, for over 15 years. She is the author of the *Tuttle Compact Indonesian Dictionary* and has edited a number of other publications on Indonesian language learning, as well as a Sundanese dictionary.

EASY
Indonesian

Learn to speak **Indonesian** quickly!

Thomas G. Oey

Revised by Katherine Davidsen

TUTTLE Publishing

Tokyo | Rutland, Vermont | Singapore

The Tuttle Story: "Books to Span the East and West"

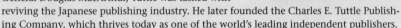

Most people are surprised to learn that the world's largest publisher of books on Asia had its humble beginnings in the tiny American state of Vermont. The company's founder, Charles E. Tuttle, belonged to a New England family steeped in publishing. And his first love was naturally books—especially old and rare editions.

Immediately after WW II, serving in Tokyo under General Douglas MacArthur, Tuttle was tasked with reviving the Japanese publishing industry. He later founded the Charles E. Tuttle Publishing Company, which thrives today as one of the world's leading independent publishers.

Though a westerner, Tuttle was hugely instrumental in bringing a knowledge of Japan and Asia to a world hungry for information about the East. By the time of his death in 1993, Tuttle had published over 6,000 books on Asian culture, history and art—a legacy honored by the Japanese emperor with the "Order of the Sacred Treasure," the highest tribute Japan can bestow upon a non-Japanese.

With a backlist of 1,500 titles, Tuttle Publishing is more active today than at any time in its past—inspired by Charles Tuttle's core mission to publish fine books to span the East and West and provide a greater understanding of each.

Published by Tuttle Publishing, an imprint of Periplus Editions (HK) Ltd.

www.tuttlepublishing.com

Copyright © 2012 Periplus Editions (HK) Ltd.
Cover photo © Odua Images/Shutterstock

ISBN: 978-0-8048-4313-3

First edition
15 14 13 12   5 4 3 2 1   1301MP

Distributed by

North America, Latin America & Europe
Tuttle Publishing
364 Innovation Drive, North Clarendon,
VT 05759-9436, USA
Tel: 1 (802) 773 8930; Fax: 1 (802) 773 6993
info@tuttlepublishing.com
www.tuttlepublishing.com

Japan
Tuttle Publishing
Yaekari Building 3rd Floor, 5-4-12 Osaki
Shinagawa-ku, Tokyo 1410032, Japan
Tel: (81) 3 5437 0171; Fax: (81) 3 5437 0755
sales@tuttle.co.jp
www.tuttle.co.jp

Asia Pacific
Berkeley Books Pte Ltd
61 Tai Seng Avenue #02-12
Singapore 534167
Tel: (65) 6280 1330; Fax: (65) 6280 6290
inquiries@periplus.com.sg
www.periplus.com

Indonesia
PT Java Books Indonesia
Jl. Rawa Gelam IV No. 9
Kawasan Industri Pulogadung
Jakarta 13930, Indonesia
Tel: 62 (21) 4682 1088; Fax: 62 (21) 461 0206
crm@periplus.co.id
www.periplus.com

Printed in Singapore

TUTTLE PUBLISHING® is a registered trademark of Tuttle Publishing, a division of Periplus Editions (HK) Ltd.

Contents

PART FIVE: Eating and Drinking

PART SIX: Happy Shopping

PART SEVEN: Things You Should Know

Bilingual Dictionaries

Introduction

Indonesian (*Bahasa Indonesia*) is a relatively new spoken and written dialect of the Malay language, developed by Dutch scholars at the beginning of the 20th century as the standard or "correct" dialect to be taught in the colonial schools. It is an Austronesian (Malayo-Polynesian) tongue of amazing complexity, rich in vocabulary borrowed from Sanskrit, Arabic, Portuguese, Dutch, English, Chinese, Javanese, and many other languages.

A colloquial *pasar* or market form of the language has been in use as the lingua franca throughout the archipelago for several centuries, and is quite simple to learn. This book is intended for visitors who wish to gain a working knowledge of colloquial Indonesian. Most visitors will find that a little study of a few words and phrases goes a very long way, and that most Indonesians are very happy to help you learn the language.

The lessons are prioritized, with more important words and phrases being given first, so that you may profit no matter how deeply into the book you go. By studying the first section only, you acquire a basic "survival" Indonesian, and by mastering the first three sections you should be able to get around quite well on your own. In order to present each lesson clearly as a unit, we have found it necessary in some cases to repeat vocabulary.

I do not apologize for preferring colloquial to "standard" or "book" Indonesian here, as this is the common spoken form of the language, and therefore the most readily understood. Care has been taken to include only vocabulary that has immediate practical application for visitors. By learning vocabulary items and practising the phrases, you will quickly gain a grasp of the language's basic elements. Rather than include long and tedious lists of words and phrases in the lessons themselves, we have appended at the back of the book a miniature bilingual dictionary that should be adequate for the needs of most tourists.

At the end of the book you will also find additional information on the use of verb and noun affixes, and suggestions for further study. Do not be deceived by the myth that "Indonesian has no grammar." As one studies the language in greater depth, one realizes how complex it actually is. After several months or years, you may realize that while you are able to get by when speaking the language, it is as difficult as any other language to truly master. In fact the grammar, morphology, and syntax of the standard Indonesian taught in schools is as complex as any other language! While it is relatively easy to communicate at a very basic level in Indonesian, top-level proficiency requires dedication and effort.

Thomas G. Oey, Ph.D.

Acknowledgements

I would like to thank my brother Eric, who originally suggested that I write this book, made many valuable suggestions, and edited the final manuscript. I would also like to thank my parents, Tom and Berenice; my aunt and uncle in Java, Tante Inggawati and Om Sutantho; the employees of Java Books and Java Engineering, who read portions of the draft and suggested many improvements; and Sudarno Sumarto, who read the draft in its final stages.

PART ONE

The Basics

Pronouncing Indonesian Correctly

To learn to pronounce the language correctly, listen carefully to the CD accompanying this book, or to native speakers of Indonesian. Try to imitate their pronunciation as accurately as you can. Be aware, however, that there are many dialectical variations in Indonesian, some producing very strong accents. As a rule, stress is generally placed on the penultimate syllable.

Unlike English, the spelling of Indonesian is consistently phonetic. The pronunciation is similar to Spanish or Italian.

Consonants

1.01 Most are pronounced roughly as in English. The main exceptions are as follows:

c is pronounced *ch* (formerly spelled "tj")
> *cari* to look for, seek   *cinta* to love

g is always hard, as in "girl":
> *guna* to use   *gila* crazy

h is very soft, and often not pronounced between different vowels:
> *habis* ⇒ *abis* finished   *hidup* ⇒ *idup* to live
> *sudah* ⇒ *suda* already   *mudah* ⇒ *muda* easy
> *lihat* ⇒ *liat* to see   *tahu* ⇒ *tau* to know

kh is found in words of Arabic derivation, and sounds like the *ch* in the Scottish word "loch":

    khusus special   *akhir* end

ng is always soft, as in "hanger":

    dengar hear   *hilang* lost

ngg is always hard, as in "hunger":

    ganggu bother   *mangga* mango

r is trilled or rolled, as in Spanish:

    ratus hundred   *baru* new

Vowels

There are six vowels (*a, e, é, i, o, u*) and two diphthongs (*ai, au*):

a is short, like the *a* in "father":

    satu one   *bayar* pay

e is usually unaccented (shwa), like the *u* in "but":

    empat four   *beli* to buy

But occasionally, *é* sounds like the *é* in "passé":

    désa village   *cabé* chili pepper

This book denotes this sound with an accent (´); however this is not used in standard written Indonesian.

i is like the *ea* in "bean":

    tiga three   *lima* five

o is as in "so":

    bodoh stupid   *boléh* may

u is like the *u* in "humor":

    tujuh seven   *untuk* for

ai is pronounced like the word "eye":

> *pantai* beach   *sampai* to reach

au is like the *ow* in "how":

> *atau* or   *pulau* island

Notes:

Under the influence of Javanese, final *ai* is often pronounced like *é* in "passé":

> *sampai* ⇒ *sampé* beach

Similarly, final *au* often becomes *o*:

> *hijau* ⇒ *hijo* green

Under the influence of the Jakarta dialect, final syllable between consonants often becomes a short *e* (shwa):

> *pintar* ⇒ *pinter* smart
>
> *benar* ⇒ *bener* true, correct
>
> *malas* ⇒ *males* lazy

Greetings

1.02

When greeting and taking leave of one another, Indonesians shake hands lightly (not firmly, the way Americans do). Muslims touch the right hand to their heart afterwards as a gesture of goodwill. (Never use the left hand to greet or touch someone.) Kissing, hugging or other physical greetings are rarely practiced in public.

Selamat is a word used in most Indonesian greetings. It comes from the Arabic *salam*, meaning peace, safety or salvation. By itself, the exclamation *Selamat!* means "Congratulations!" Like English "good," it is followed by the time of day and other words to form most common greetings:

Selamat datang	Welcome (*datang* = to come)
Selamat pagi	Good morning (*pagi* = morning, until 11 am)
Selamat siang	Good day (*siang* = midday, from 11 am to 3 pm)
Selamat soré	Good afternoon (*soré* = late afternoon, 3 pm to nightfall)

Selamat malam	Good evening (*malam* = night, after dark)
Selamat tidur	Good night (*tidur* = to sleep)

Apa kabar is another common greeting which literally means "What news?" (*apa* = what, *kabar* = news), or in other words "How are you?" The standard answer is "*Kabar baik*," meaning "I'm fine" (*baik* = well, fine).

You will also find yourself greeted with the following questions, even by complete strangers:

Mau ke mana? (lit: Want-to-where?)	Where are you going?
Dari mana? (lit: From-where?)	Where are you [coming] from?

This is said out of curiosity, and the person is usually not all that interested where you are actually going or coming from. This is just another way of saying "Hello!"

You may answer:

Dari [+ place]	From [+ place]
Saya mau ke [+ place]	I am going to [+ place]
Jalan-jalan saja. (lit: Walk-walk-only.)	Just going for a walk.
Tidak ke mana-mana. (lit: Not-to-where-where.)	Not anywhere in particular.

When taking leave of someone, it is polite to excuse oneself by saying:

Mari. Saya pergi dulu. (lit: Let's. I-go-first.)	I am going now. (= Goodbye for now!)
Sampai jumpa lagi. (lit: Until-meet-again.)	See you again.

More informally, you can also say:

> *Da!* or *Bye!*   Goodbye (so long!)

 Note: *Da!* comes from the Dutch *dag* meaning "day" (also used as a farewell). *Bye* is from English.

If you are the one staying behind, you respond by saying:

> **Selamat jalan.**   "Bon voyage"
> (lit: Safe-journey.)

Forms of Address

1.03 As in any language, there are many ways of addressing someone in Indonesian. Because Indonesians have a strong sense of social hierarchy, these forms of address often carry with them certain class and other distinctions. It is important therefore to use the appropriate term. Some forms of address are quite "safe" or "neutral" in this regard, and may be used in a wide variety of situations; these are the ones that should be learned first and used most often.

Bapak or *pak* (literally: "father") is the most common way of addressing an adult male in Indonesian. It is used very much like "Mr." or "sir" in English. *Bapak* is always used when addressing older men, and may also be used to address a contemporary or a younger man (although other forms may be used in this case as well, see below).

Ibu or *bu* (literally: "mother") is similarly used to address all women, particularly older, married women.

 Note: *Bapak* and *ibu* are often used followed by the person's first name, meaning Mr. or Mrs. So-and-so. This is quite universal throughout Indonesia, and you can almost never go wrong addressing someone in this way (except when you are much older than the person you are addressing).

Anda is a term of fairly recent coinage, intended to mean "you" in a neutral way. It is also considered to be rather formal and is likewise used among educated adults who meet for the first time (also in television commercials, etc.).

Kamu and *engkau* are pronouns that both mean "you" in a familiar sense (equivalent to *Du* in German or *tu* in French). They are used in informal situations to address close friends, children or social inferiors, but should not generally be used as a substitute for English "you." Once you get to know someone well, you can use their name or the form *kamu* ("you"). Generally speaking, personal pronouns such as "you" equivalents can be left out in colloquial Indonesian.

Tuan ("sir"), *nyonya* ("madam"), and *nona* ("miss") are forms that Indonesians may use to address you. *Tuan* means "master" and was used to address aristocrats and Europeans during colonial times. *Nyonya* and *nona* are borrowed from the Portuguese. As a foreign visitor, you may only ever hear these used for you—you will not need to use them yourself.

Om ("Uncle") and *Tante* ("Aunt") are borrowed from Dutch and are used to address older men or women, especially if they are not blood relations.

Mas literally means "older brother" in Javanese, and is a polite form of address for a contemporary or a younger person. It is commonly used in Java to address a waiter, porter or pedicab (*bécak*) driver, and hence can have the connotation of addressing a social inferior. When in doubt it is better to stick with *Pak*. *Bang* can be used in Jakarta or Sumatra.

Mbak (*Kak* in Sumatra) is similarly used in Java to summon a waitress or a shopgirl.

Summary

To be on the safe side, always use *bapak* and *ibu* when addressing adults whom you are meeting for the first time (*anda* may also be used by younger people to address their peers). Once you get to know someone better, use *bapak* or *ibu* followed by the person's first name, or (if you are roughly the same age) simply the first name alone.

The following is a brief dialogue between a foreigner (F) and an Indonesian (I) who works in a hotel.

I: *Selamat pagi!*	Good morning.
F: *Selamat pagi!*	Good morning, *pak*.
I: *Mau ke mana?*	Where are you going?
F: *Saya mau ke restoran.*	I'm going to the restaurant.

Pronouns

On the whole, Indonesians do not use the word "you" as we do in English. First names (often preceded by kinship terms like *Pak*) may be used, or the context may make it obvious.

	singular	plural
1st person	I *saya, aku*	we *kita, kami*
2nd person	you *anda, kamu, engkau bapak, ibu*	you all *kalian, sekalian, anda sekalian*
3rd person	he, she, it *dia*	they *meréka*

Note: Indonesian pronouns do not distinguish gender. Thus *dia* may mean "he, she," or "it."

1st person (singular): I *saya, **aku***

The pronoun ***saya*** originally meant "your slave" but now generally means "I". ***Aku*** also means "I" but is used in more informal circumstances, as are the Jakarta slang forms *gua* and *gué* (which derive from Hokkien Chinese). Note that words for "I" are often omitted because this is understood.

1st person (plural): we ***kita, kami***

Kami means "we" or "us" but formally excludes the person or persons being addressed, whereas ***kita*** includes the person or persons you are speaking to. In everyday speech, *kita* is in fact used in both contexts and you may generally use this form to translate English "we."

2nd person (singular): you
anda, kamu, engkau, bapak, ibu

As a sign of respect, especiallly to elders, use *bapak* or *ibu*. In informal circumstances, the first name alone may also be used. If the person being addressed is about the same age as yourself, use ***anda*** or their first name. ***Kamu*** or ***engkau*** may be used for children or if you know the person well.

2nd person (plural): you all ***kalian, sekalian, anda sekalian***

3rd person (singular): he, she, it ***dia***

For animate objects and persons use ***dia***. The word ***beliau*** is also used in formal circumstances to refer to a person of very high status who is not present. For inanimate things, use ***ini*** (this) or ***itu*** (that), to mean "it."

3rd person (plural): they ***meréka***

1.05

Basic Vocabulary

The following are essential words for basic "survival" Indonesian. We suggest that you make a set of flashcards to help yourself learn them quickly.

tidak no, not
ada have, there is
bisa can
datang arrive
pergi go, leave
jalan walk, travel; street
sini here
dalam in
makan eat
beli buy
harga price
mahal expensive
lagi again, more
cukup enough
terlalu too
banyak much, many
lebih greater, more
habis gone, finished
jauh far
hari day
pagi morning
hotél hotel
bagus good (of objects)
baik good (of qualities)
besar big
sudah already

ya yes
mau want; going to
lihat see
dari from
ke to, toward
di in, at
sana there
luar out
minum drink
jual sell
bayar pay
murah cheap
uang money
sekarang now
semua all
sedikit few, little
kurang fewer, less
masih still
dekat near
malam night
siang day, afternoon
  (11 am – 3 pm)
mobil car
jelék bad
kecil small
belum not yet

Questions

As in English, interrogative words and phrases are used to form questions:

Apa?	What?
Apa ini?	What is this?
Siapa?	Who?
Kalau...?	What about...?
Kapan?	When?
Kenapa?	Why? Pardon?
Di mana?	Where?
Bagaimana?	How?
(Yang) mana?	Which one?
Kemana?	To where?
Dari mana?	From where?

Kapan datang di sini? When did you arrive here?
(lit: When-arrive-at-here?)

Dari mana? Where are you from?
(lit: From-where?)

Siapa namanya? What is your (his, her) name?
(lit: Who-the name?)

Bagaimana saya bisa...? How can I...?
(lit: How-I-can-...?)

Kenapa tidak bisa...? Why can't I...?
(lit: Why-not-can-...?)

Mau ke mana? Where are you going?
(lit: Want-to-where?)

Kalau ini bagaimana? What about this one?
(lit: If-this-how?)

Di mana...? Where is...?
(lit: At-where-...?)

Dimana kamar kecil/W.C.? Where is the restroom/WC?
(lit: At-where-small room/toilet?)

Note: *WC* is pronounced "way-say": ***pria*** = men's; ***wanita*** = ladies'

The above question words do not always have to be used in order to ask a question. The fact that you are posing a question can also be clear from the context or by using a rising intonation at the end of the sentence. To be even more clear, you may also introduce the question with ***apakah***, which makes the following statement a question.

Apakah *masih ada...?* Do you still have any...?
(lit: ?-still-have...?)

Apakah *di sini ada...?* Do you have any ... here?
(lit: ?-at here-have...?)

Simple Phrases

The following are simple sentences that will be used often, and should be memorized.

> *Ada...?* Is there any...? Do you have any? Are there any...?
> (lit: Have...?)
>
> *Saya mau...* I would like ... I want to...
> (lit: I-want...)
>
> *Tidak mau!* I don't want to! I don't want any!
>
> *Saya mau pergi ke...* I want to go to...
> (lit: I-want-go-to-...)
>
> *Saya mau minum...* I would like to drink some...
> (lit: I-want-drink-...)
>
> *Saya mau makan...* I would like to eat some...
> (lit: I-want-eat-...)
>
> *Saya mau beli ini/itu...* I want to buy this/that...
> (lit: I-want-buy-this/that.)
>
> *Berapa harganya?* How much does it cost?/What is the price?
> (lit: How much-its price?)
>
> *Saya mau bayar.* I want to pay.
> (lit: I-want-pay.)

Terlalu mahal! Too expensive!

Tidak bisa! Not possible!

When you interrupt or pass by someone, you should say:

Permisi! Excuse me!

When an actual apology is required, use:

Ma'af! or *Sori!* I'm sorry!

Ma'af, saya tidak mengerti. I'm sorry, I don't (or didn't)
(lit: Sorry, I-not-understand.) understand.

Bapak Peter mau makan sekarang? Do you want to eat now,
(lit: Mr. Peter-want-eat-now?) Peter?

Ibu Susan mau pergi sekarang? Do you want to go now,
(lit: Mrs. Susan-want-go-now?) Susan?

Note: You may find it strange that Indonesians refer to you in English as "Mr. Peter" and "Mrs. Susan" (especially if you are not married!), but this simply reflects that many Indonesians feel uncomfortable addressing someone (especially a foreigner or visitor) without a title.

Requests

Requests may be made in a number of different ways. Note that the English word "please" has no direct equivalent in Indonesian, and is translated differently depending upon the circumstances and the type of request that is being made. These various translations of "please" should not be confused.

Tolong literally means "to help." It is used to politely introduce a request when you are asking someone to do something for you.

Tolong panggil taksi. Please (help me) call a taxi.
(lit: Help-call-taxi.)

Boléh means "allowed" and is used in the sense of "May I please..." when asking politely to see or do something, for example in a shop.

>*Boléh saya lihat ini?* May I see this please?
>(lit: May-I-see-this?)
>
>*Boléh saya bicara dengan...?* May I speak with... please?
>(lit: May-I-speak-with...?)
>
>*Boléh saya lihat itu?* May I look at that please?
>(lit: May-I-see-that?)

Minta means "request" and is a polite way of asking for things like food or drink in a restaurant. Note that the use of *saya* (meaning "I") beforehand is optional.

>*Minta air minum.* [I] would like some drinking water please.
>(lit: Ask-water-drink.)
>
>*Saya minta nasi goréng.* I would like some fried rice please.
>(lit: I-ask-fried rice.)

Saya pesan is another way of prefacing a request, and means simply "I would like to order some..."

>*Saya pesan nasi goreng.* I would like to order some fried rice.
>(lit: 1-order-fried rice.)

Kasih means "give," and is a somewhat more colloquial and informal way of ordering something. It is also used after *tolong* to politely request a specific item or specific quantity of something.

>*Tolong kasih air minum.*
>(lit: Give-water-to drink.)
>Please give me some drinking water.
>
>*Tolong kasih itu.* Please give me that one.
>(lit: Help-give-that.)
>
>*Tolong kasih dua.* Please give me two [of them].
>(lit: Help-give-two.)

Coba means "try (on)" and is also used with verbs such as *lihat* ("see") in the sense of "Please may I see..." when asking to look at something in a shop window or a display case, for example:

> *Coba lihat itu.* Please let me have a look at that.
> (lit: Try-see-that.)

Silakan means "Please go ahead!" or "Be my guest!" and is used by a host to invite his or her guests to do something, or as a response to a request for permission to do something. It is, for example, polite to wait for an Indonesian host or hostess to say *Silakan!* before trying any drinks or snacks that have been placed before you. (Please note that *silakan* is never used when requesting something.)

Silakan masuk!	Please come in!
Silakan duduk!	Please sit down!
Silakan minum!	Please drink!
Silakan makan!	Please eat!
Boléh saya masuk?	May I come in?
Silakan!	Please do!

Terima kasih is used to say "thank you." It also is used to mean "no thank you" when refusing something being offered. Indonesians tend to use it much less often than it is used in English.

Terima kasih
Thank you

Sama-sama! ("same-same") or *Kembali!* ("return") are the normal responses to *terima kasih*, both meaning "You're welcome."

Numbers

Ordinal Numbers

se- prefix indicating one

puluh ten, multiples of ten

belas teen

ratus hundred

ribu thousand

juta million

milyar billion

nol, kosong zero

satu one		*sebelas* eleven
dua two		*dua belas* twelve
tiga three		*tiga belas* thirteen
empat four		*empat belas* fourteen
lima five		*lima belas* fifteen
enam six		*enam belas* sixteen
tujuh seven		*tujuh belas* seventeen
delapan eight		*delapan belas* eighteen
sembilan nine		*sembilan belas* nineteen
sepuluh ten		

dua puluh	twenty	*tiga puluh*	thirty
dua puluh satu	twenty-one	*empat puluh*	forty
dua puluh dua	twenty-two	*lima puluh*	fifty
dua puluh tiga	twenty-three	*enam puluh*	sixty
dua puluh empat	twenty-four	*tujuh puluh*	seventy
dua puluh lima	twenty-five	*delapan puluh*	eighty
dua puluh enam	twenty-six	*sembilan puluh*	ninety
dua puluh tujuh	twenty-seven		etc.

seratus	one hundred
dua ratus	two hundred
tiga ratus	three hundred
	etc.
seratus lima belas	one hundred fifteen
dua ratus sembilan puluh	two hundred ninety
tujuh ratus tiga puluh enam	seven hundred thirty-six

seribu	one thousand
dua ribu	two thousand
tiga ribu	three thousand
	etc.
seribu lima ratus	one thousand five hundred
sembilan ribu sebelas	nine thousand eleven
delapan ratus ribu	eight hundred thousand

Cardinal numbers

Cardinal numbers are formed by attaching the prefix *ke* to any ordinal number (with the exception of *pertama*, "first"). The word *yang* meaning "which" may also be added when no noun is mentioned, to convey the sense of "the first one" (literally: "the one which is first"), "the second one" and so forth.

(yang) pertama (the) first

(yang) kedua (the) second

(yang) ketiga (the) third

(yang) keempat (the) fourth

(yang) kelima (the) fifth

etc.

(yang) terakhir (the) last

Fractions

setengah, separuh	one half
sepertiga	one third
seperempat	one quarter
tiga per empat	three fourths
dua per lima	two fifths
dua setengah	two and a half

Money

Note: The Indonesian unit of currency is the Rupiah, abbreviated as Rp.

Harga ini berapa, bu? What is the price of this, Bu?

Enam ratus lima puluh rupiah. Rp650.

Tiga ribu tujuh ratus lima puluh rupiah. Rp3.750.

Delapan puluh lima ribu lima ratus rupiah. Rp85.500.

Seratus lima puluh lima ribu rupiah. Rp155.000.

Etiquette and Body Language

In Indonesia, body language is as much a part of effective communication as speech. By it you may either quickly offend or put someone at ease.

Indonesians may tolerate shorts and T-shirts in tourist shops, hotels and at the beach, but not in their homes or places of worship. It is customary to wear long pants and a shirt with a collar for men, long pants or a skirt below the knees and a blouse with sleeves for women, when going out in public. Sarongs, short pants and T-shirts are only worn around the house. In Bali, a colored sash must be worn tied around the waist when entering a temple.

Avoid using the left hand. Indonesians use their right hand to eat with and their left hand to do their business!

Point with the thumb, never with the index finger. Raise or nod your head instead of pointing at people.

It is not polite to put your hands on your hips, or to cross your arms in front of you when speaking to someone.

Footwear should be taken off *(ditanggal)* when visiting an Indonesian home. Slippers or sandals are acceptable at all but the most formal of occasions.

Avoid exposing the sole of your foot at someone.

Avoid touching the head or slapping someone on the back.

Indonesians are not accustomed to public displays of affection (hugging and kissing).

Beckon someone with the hand by waving with fingers together and the palm facing downwards.

Javanese will often stoop or bend over slightly when passing you. This is based on the traditional custom in the Javanese *kraton* or palace, where the level of one's head is equated with one's social status. Servants were formerly expected to walk with their legs squat, crab-like.

Indonesians bathe at least twice daily, before breakfast and supper, and may find it very strange if you do not do the same! A common greeting in the evening is *Sudah mandi belum?* ("Have you had your bath yet?") Nothing in particular is meant by this, it is simply another way of saying "Hello!"

When visiting an Indonesian home, it is normal to greet the head of the household first. Greetings can be somewhat long and complicated. It is polite to shake hands, and to nod the head and state one's name while doing so. You will be expected to meet all adults in the house, and to go through a litany of "Small Talk" questions and answers (see Part Three below).

Wait for the signal *Silakan!* before entering, sitting, eating or drinking. Never completely finish food or drink presented to you, as to do so is to request more. Wait for your host or hostess to offer.

When you leave, say goodbye to all adults in the house, shake hands again and tell them where you are going and why you must leave so soon. Often you will be asked to stay longer, eat, bathe, take a nap, or spend the night when you were not expecting to! These elaborate rituals reinforce the atmosphere of congeniality in Indonesian society and such invitations are not to be taken seriously unless they are repeated several times. Always decline an invitation gracefully the first time, as the person making it is perhaps just being polite and doesn't really expect you to accept.

Outbursts and public displays of emotion or displeasure are to be avoided at all costs.

PART TWO

A Quick Word About Grammar

Verbs

The verb is the heart of the Indonesian sentence. The following is a list of verbs that are commonly used in everyday speech. You will probably learn them quickly, since they will come up again and again.

ada be, have, exist	*bicara* speak
mau want (= will)	*perlu* need
bisa be able to (= can)	*tahu* know
suka like	*punya* own
dapat get, reach, attain	*jadi* become
harus necessary	
boléh permitted, allowed to (= may)	

Common verbs of motion (intransitive)

datang come, arrive   *duduk* sit

ikut accompany, go along   *jalan* walk, travel

keluar go out, exit   *masuk* go in, enter

pergi go   *berhenti* stop

pulang go back [home]   *kembali* return

turun come down, get off (a bus, etc.)

mulai begin   *lari* run

Common verbs of action (transitive)

ambil take, get   *bawa* carry

beli buy   *cari* look for, seek

dengar hear   *kasih* give

lihat see   *naik* ride, go up, climb up

pakai use, wear   *séwa* rent

taruh put, place   *terima* receive

The verb "to be"

 Note: That the English verb "to be" does not really exist in Indonesian. Sentences of the sort **X is Y** in English are expressed by simply juxtaposing X with Y. The verb "to be" is then understood.

Saya orang Amérika. I [am] an American.

Hotél itu mahal. That hotel [is] expensive.

Réstoran ini bagus. This restaurant [is] good.

Adalah may sometimes be used to join two nouns in the sense of **X is Y** although this is usually optional. (*Adalah* cannot be used in this way, however, to join a noun with an adjective.)

Saya adalah *orang Inggris.* I *am* a Briton.

Dia adalah *orang yang cerdik.* He *is* a clever person.

Word order

The standard or basic word order of Indonesian sentences is the same as in English, namely: **subject + verb + object + complement.**

Saya perlu taksi. I need a taxi.

Saya perlu taksi bésok pagi.
I need a taxi tomorrow morning.

Kita cari hotél. We are looking for a hotel.

Saya mau séwa kamar. I want to rent a room.

John datang kemarin. John arrived yesterday.

Dia berangkat ke Bali bésok.
He will leave for Bali tomorrow.

There is one very basic difference, however. In Indonesian, the most important noun or "topic" of the sentence is normally placed first. If the topic of the sentence happens to be the object of the verb, then this will be placed first and the "passive form" of the verb with *di-* will often be used (see below).

Bapak mau ke mana? Where is Bapak going?
(lit: Father-want-to-where?)

Buku itu ditaruh di sana. Put the book over there.
(lit: Book-that-is put-at-there.)

Buah ini dimakan.   This fruit is to be eaten.
(lit: Fruit-this-to be eaten.)   (i.e. "Go ahead and eat this fruit!")

Very often the subject of a sentence is omitted, as it is clear from the context.

Mau pergi? Do [*you*] want to go?

Ada kamar? Do [*you*] have any rooms?

Minta air minum. [*I*] would like some drinking water.

Boléh lihat? May [*I*] see?

Verb forms

2.03 The most common form of a verb is the "active" prefix *me-*. However, this is commonly omitted in everyday conversation. For further information on these verbal affixes, see Appendix A.

Saya mau melihat Borobudur. I want to see Borobudur.

Saya mau lihat Borobudur. (same)

The passive form *di–*

The passive form of a transitive verb is formed with the prefix *di-*. Note that the passive form often implies an imperative.

*Sepatu ini boléh di***coba***.* The shoes may be tried on.
> (i.e. "You may try on the shoes.")

*Di***coba** *dulu!* Try it/them [on] first!

*Nasi ini di***masak***.* This rice is to be cooked.
> (i.e. "Cook this rice!")

Tense

2.04

Verbs do not change their form to indicate tense, and the same form of the verb is used to speak of the past, present and future. Usually it is clear from the context which is intended. To be more specific, auxiliary verbs and words indicating a specific time reference may be added, just as in English.

Saya makan. I eat. I am eating.

Saya **sedang** *makan.* I am eating.

Saya **sudah** *makan.* I have *already* eaten.

Saya makan **tadi.** I ate *just* now.

Saya **akan** *makan.* I *will* eat.

Saya (akan) makan **nanti.** I will eat *later*.

Present tense

If no auxiliary verb or specific time reference is used, it is generally assumed that one is speaking about the present.

Sekarang ("now") is used to emphasize the fact that one is speaking about the present.

Kita pergi sekarang. We are leaving *now*.

Saya mau makan sekarang. I want to eat *now*.

Sedang is another auxiliary verb used in the sense of "to be in the middle of" doing something:

Saya sedang makan. I am *(in the middle of)* eating.

Kita sedang bicara. We are *(in the middle of)* speaking.

Future tense

Akan ("shall, will") is an auxiliary verb used to express the future.

Tahun depan saya akan kembali lagi ke Indonésia.
Next year I *will* return to Indonesia again.

Mau ("to want to") is often used as an auxiliary verb to signify the near future, just as in English. It is then followed by the main verb. In this case it often has the sense of "to intend to, will" do something.

Bésok saya mau pergi kecandi Borobudur.
Tomorrow I *want to* [intend to, will] go to the Borobudur temple.

Nanti ("later") is also used as a specific time reference indicating future tense, often after *mau* + **verb:**

Saya (akan) pergi nanti. I will go *later*.

Saya mau pergi nanti. I intend to go *later*.

Past tense

2.05

Sudah ("already") is used in Indonesian to indicate most forms of the past tense in English. It is placed before the verb, and is often not translated in English.

> *Dia* sudah *pergi?* Has he gone *already?*
>
> *Ya, dia* sudah *pergi.* Yes, he has gone *already.*
>
> *Saya sudah satu bulan belajar Bahasa Indonésia.*
> I have [already] been studying Indonesian one month.

Kemarin ("yesterday") and *tadi* ("just now, earlier") are specific time references used to indicate the past.

> **Kemarin** *saya bicara dengan dia.* I spoke with him/her *yesterday*
>
> *Saya datang* **tadi.** I arrived *just now.*

Past tense with *waktu* ("the time when")

Waktu ("time" or "the time when") is another time reference used to indicate actions which occurred in the past. Followed by *itu* ("that") it means "by that time" or "at that time" and indicates what in English would be a pluperfect (past perfect) tense.

> **Waktu** *dia datang, kita sedang makan.*
> *When* (at the time) he arrived, we were eating.
>
> **Waktu itu** *saya baru pulang.*
> *At that time,* I had just come home.

Waktu may also be combined with *sudah* to indicate the past perfect tense:

> **Waktu** *dia datang, kita* **sudah** *makan.*
> *When* he arrived, we had *already* eaten.
>
> **Waktu itu** *saya sudah pergi.*
> *By that time* I had already gone.

Past tense with *pernah* ("ever")

Pernah is a word meaning "been" or "ever." When placed before the main verb, like *sudah*, it expresses the past tense, but is not usually translated in English. It is commonly used together with *sudah* to emphasize past action.

> *Saya* pernah *lihat itu.* I have seen that.

> *Saya sudah* pernah *lihat itu.* I have seen that before.

Pernah is often used on its own.

> *Anda* pernah *ke sana?* Have you *ever* been there?

> *Saya* pernah *ke sana.* I have been there *before.*

When used negatively with *tidak* or *belum, pernah* has the sense of "never" or "not yet":

> *Saya* tidak pernah *makan daging.* I have *never* eaten meat.

> *Saya* belum pernah *ke sana.* I have *not yet* been there.

Negation

2.06

Tidak, meaning "not," is the most common negative word, used to negate verbs and adjectives. Spoken contracted forms of *tidak* are *ndak, gak* and *nggak/enggak.*

> *Hotél* ini *tidak bagus.* This hotel is *not* good.

> *Dia* tidak *pergi.* He/she is *not* going.

> *Kenapa John* enggak *datang?* Why *didn't* John come?

Whenever possible, however, Indonesians prefer to use *kurang* ("less") or *belum* ("not yet") instead of *tidak* because the latter seems to carry a sense of "finality" or to be too "strong." *Kurang* in this sense means "not really" or "not very":

Hotél ini *kurang baik.*
This hotel is *not very* good.

Saya kurang *suka itu.*
I don't *really* like it.

Dia kurang *mengerti.*
He *doesn't really* understand.

Kenapa Joe belum *datang?*
Why *hasn't* Joe arrived *yet?*

Belum ("not yet") is also more commonly used than *tidak*, as a response to a question involving time or action.

Dia sudah pergi? **Belum.** Has he gone? *Not yet.*

Anda sudah pernah ke Bali? **Belum.**
Have you ever been to Bali? *Not yet.*

Bukan is used to negate nouns. *Tidak* is used to negate adjectives, as explained earlier.

Bukan *ini, itu.* *Not* this (one), that (one).

Itu **bukan** *lukisan tapi batik.*
That is *not* a painting but batik.

Itu **bukan** *urusan saya.*
That is *not* my business.

Jangan! ("Don't!") is used to express negative imperatives instead of *tidak*.

Jangan *pergi!* *Don't* go!

Jangan *mau!* *Don't* want!
(lit: Don't accept it!)

Nouns

anak child	*orang* person, human being
buku book	*nama* name
makanan food	*minuman* drink
mata eye	*hari* day
mobil car	*bis* bus
kamar room	*rumah* house, home
kursi chair, seat	*méja* table
tempat place, seat	*kota* town, city
jalan street, road	*kunci* key
kawan friend	*air* water
suami husband	*isteri* wife
nasi rice (cooked)	*gelas* glass
gunung mountain	*pantai* beach
karcis ticket	*barang* goods, item
hal matter	*masalah* problem
muka face	*belakang* back
bahasa language	*negara* country
séndok spoon	*garpu* fork
piring plate	*hotél* hotel

Articles

Unlike English, Indonesian does not use any articles (a, an, the) before nouns:

> *Saya akan naik bis ke Bali.* I will take *the* bus to Bali.
>
> *Kita cari hotél yang murah.* We are looking for *a* cheap hotel.
>
> *Kita mau séwa kamar.* We want to rent *a* room.
>
> *Ada kunci?* Do you have *the* key?

The sense of the English definite article ("the") can often be conveyed, however, by the possessive suffix *-nya* (literally: "his, hers, its, yours") or by the demonstrative pronouns *ini* and *itu* ("this" and "that"):

> *Orang*nya *tinggi.* *The* person [is] tall.
>
> *Bis* **itu** *di mana?* Where is *the* [that] bus?
>
> *Batik* **ini** *mahal.* *The* [this] batik cloth is expensive.

Plural forms

Singular or plural forms of nouns are not normally distinguished, and the same form is used for both. Singular or plural are indicated instead by the context, or through the use of other words such as "all," "many," etc.

> **Semua** *orang senang.* *All* the people were pleased.
>
> **Banyak** *turis datang.* *Many* tourists arrived.

Reduplicating a noun may emphasize that it is plural:

> *anak-anak* (also written *anak2*) children
>
> *buku-buku* books

However, reduplication often carries the meaning "a variety of." It is also used to create new words with very different meanings from the simple forms. It is best therefore to avoid reduplication to indicate the plural unless you know what you are saying.

> *mala* eye *mata-mata* spy
>
> *semata-mata* only, exclusively

Para indicates plural for persons, often in a formal context:

> **para** *penumpang* passengers
>
> **para** *penonton* viewers

Note: More information concerning noun formation using prefixes and suffixes is given at the back of this book.

Classifier words

A number cannot be placed before many Indonesian nouns without the use of certain "classifier words" between the number and the noun. This is like the use of words in English such as "two *pieces* of cake" or "three *sheets* of paper," etc. Some of the more common classifiers are listed below.

> *batang* (lit: "trunk") used for cigarettes, trees, etc.: *sepuluh* **batang** *rokok* ten cigarettes

> *biji* (lit: "seed") used for small objects; in slang, a counter for any object

> *buah* (lit: "fruit") used for larger and abstract things; or a general counter for inanimate objects

> *ékor* (lit: "tail") used for animals: *dua* **ekor** *ayam* [or *ayam dua* ekor] two chickens

> *hélai* (lit: "sheet") used for paper

> *lembar* (lit: "sheet") used for paper, wood, etc.

> *orang* (lit: "person") used for people: *tiga* **orang** *dokter* three doctors

> *potong* (lit: "cut") used for slices of bread, cloth, etc.: *dua* **potong** *roti* two slices of bread

> *pucuk* (lit: "sprout") used for letters: *lima* **pucuk** *surat* five letters

> *tusuk* (lit: "stick") used for satay

Adjectives

Some common adjectives are listed below together with their opposites.

baru new	*lama* old (of things)
muda young	*tua* old (of persons)
baik, bagus good	*jelek* bad, ugly
besar big	*kecil* small
mahal expensive	*murah* cheap
tinggi tall, high (height)	*péndék* short
panjang long (length)	*lébar* wide (width)
pelan slow	*cepat* fast
penuh full	*kosong* empty
sama the same	*lain* different
ringan light	*berat* heavy
mudah, gampang easy	*susah, sukar* difficult

Noun modifiers such as adjectives and possessives always follow the word being modified, with the relative pronoun *yang* (meaning "[the one] which") sometimes used (see below):

mobil baru new car

mobil yang baru the new car (lit: "the car which is new")

gadis (yang) muda (the) young girl

orang (yang) baik (the) good person

gedung (yang) tinggi (the) high building

buku saya my book

rumah bapak your house (lit: "father's house")

anak dia or *anaknya* his/their child (*-nya = dia*)

negeri kita our country

Comparatives and superlatives

	COMPARATIVES	SUPERLATIVES
baik	*lebih baik*	*paling baik*
good	better	best
cepat	*lebih cepat*	*paling cepat*
fast	faster	fastest
tinggi	*lebih tinggi*	*paling tinggi*
tall	taller	tallest

Lebih ("more") and *kurang* ("less") are used with adjectives to form comparatives. If the thing being compared to is mentioned, this follows the word *daripada* ("than") or *dibandingkan* ("compared to").

Dia lebih *pintar.* He/she is cleverer.

Dia lebih *pintar* daripada *saya.* He/she is cleverer than I.

Madé lebih *muda* daripada *Peter.*
Made is younger than Peter.

Hotél ini lebih *baik* daripada *itu.*
This hotel is better than that one.

Dia lebih *tinggi* daripada *saya.* She/he is taller than I am.

Bis ini lebih *cepat* daripada *itu.*
This bus is faster than that one.

Ini kurang *baik.* This one is not so good.

Ini kurang *baik* dibandingkan *itu.*
This [one] is not as good as that [one].

Adam kurang *tinggi* dibandingkan *John.*
Adam is not as tall as John. (lit: "less tall compared to John")

 Note: *Daripada* is often shortened to *dari.*

Batik ini lebih mahal dari *itu.*
This batik cloth is more expensive than that one.

Paling ("the most") is used to form the superlatives "most, -est."
Another way is to add the prefix *ter-.*

paling *baik,* ter*baik* the best

paling *mahal,* ter*mahal* the most expensive

paling *baru,* ter*baru* the newest

 Note: The reduplicated form *paling-paling* means "at most":

Ke Semarang paling-paling *dua jam.*
To (get to) Semarang takes at most two hours.

Equality

2.12 Equality is expressed by the prefix *se-* ("the same as") plus an adjective.

Dia setinggi saya. He is *the same* height *as* I.

The construction *-nya sama* after a noun also expresses equality.

*Harga*nya sama. The prices are *the same.*

*Umur*nya sama. (Our, their) ages are *the same.*

*Tinggi*nya sama. (Our, their) heights are *the same.*

*Warna*nya sama. The colors are *the same.*

Possessives

2.13 Like adjectives, possessives follow the noun they modify:

> *Ini buku(nya) Eric.* This is *Eric's* book.
>
> *Ini rumuh saya.* This is *my* house.
>
> *Sudah sampai di hotél Bapak.*
> We have reached *your* (Bapak's) hotel.

Punya "to own, belong to" is a transitive verb that can be used to emphasize the relation of possession and make it clearer who owns what. It gives a sense of belonging to nouns.

> *Ini* **punya** *saya.* This belongs to me.
>
> *Mobil itu* **punya** *siapa?*
> Who owns that car?
>
> *Nyoman* **punya** *tiga isteri.*
> Nyoman has three wives.
>
> *Orang itu tidak* **punya** *uang.*
> That person has no money.

The abbreviated forms of personal pronouns -*ku* "my" for *aku* and -*mu* "your" for *kamu* may be suffixed to nouns, but should only be used to address persons you know very well, or children.

> *Berapa umur**mu**?* What is *your* age?
>
> *Itu harapan**ku**.* That is *my* hope.

The suffix –nya

Adding the suffix -*nya* to a noun is equivalent to placing the third person pronouns *dia* or *mereka* immediately after a noun to express possession. It therefore means "his, her, its" or "their" (sometimes also "your").

> *Ini buku John.* This is *John's* book.
>
> *Ini buku* **dia**. This is *his* (her, their) book.
>
> *Ini buku**nya***. This is *his* (her, their) book.

This suffix -*nya* is also used when a possessive would be unnecessary in English, in which case it takes the sense of the English definite pronoun "the":

> *Mobil**nya** di sana.* *The* car is over there.
>
> *Hotél**nya** di mana?* Where is *the* hotel?

Adverbs

Like adjectives, most adverbs follow the words they modify.

> *begini, beg itu* thus, so   *juga* also, too
>
> *dulu* before, first   *saja* only, just
>
> *sekali* very (also "once"; *duo kali* = "twice")

Dia **juga** *pergi.* He will go *also.*

Dia pergi **juga.** He *did* go, *eventually.*

Saya berangkat **dulu.** I am leaving *first.*

Minta air putih **saja.** I would like drinking water *only.*

Makanan ini enak **sekali.** This food is *very* tasty.

However, the following commonly used adverbs precede the verbs they modify:

belum not yet	**kira-kira** approximately	**hanya** only
cuma merely	**sangat** very, extremely	**masih** still
hampir almost	**terlalu** too (excessive)	**sudah** already

Saya masih *makan.* I am *still* eating.

Kita hampir *sampai di Solo.*
We have *almost* arrived at Solo.

Hal ini sangat *penting.*
This matter is *extremely* important.

Saya hanya *mau beli tiga buah.*
I *only* want to buy three pieces.

Barang ini terlalu *mahal!*
This item is *too* expensive!

Prepositions

Di "in," *dari* "from," and *ke* "to, toward" are the most common prepositions.

Dia ada di *rumah sekarang.* He/she is *in* the house now.

Saya jalan dari *sana.* I walked *from* there.

Saya mau ke *Bandung.* I want to go *to* Bandung.

Saya mau pergi ke *Bali.* I would like to go *to* Bali.

Di is combined with the following words to form a number of common phrases indicating location:

di sini here	**di sana, di situ** there
di dalam inside	**di luar** outside
di bawah below, downstairs	**di atas** above, upstairs
di depan in front of	**di belakang** behind
di muka in front of	**di sebelah** next (door) to
di seberang across (the street) from	

Imperatives

To form the imperative, the suffix *-lah* is added to the verb:

Pergilah! Go!   **Makan**lah! Eat!

Mari, mari kita or (more colloquially) *ayo* are used as hortatives ("come let us"):

Mari *makan*. Come, let's eat.

Mari kita *berangkat sekarang*. Come, let's depart now.

Ayo *pulang*, ayo. Come on, let's go home.

Note: The word *ayo* is very commonly used, just as in English we would say "C'mon" or "Let's go!"

The Relative Pronoun *yang*

Yang is an all-purpose relative pronoun meaning "which," "who," and "that." It is most often used in the construction:

[noun] + **yang** + *[adjective]*
the [noun] *which is* [adjective]

If a noun is not specified, it simply means "*the* [adjective] *one.*"

> *Saya cari tas* **yang** *besar.*
> I am looking for a large bag. (lit: "a bag which is large")

> *Saya cari hotel* **yang** *murah.*
> I am looking for a cheap hotel. (lit: "a hotel which is cheap")

> **Yang** *hitam?* The black one?

> *Bukan,* **yang** *mérah.* No, the red one.

You may hear **yang mana**, which is not strictly grammatical.

> *Ibu mau* **yang mana?**
> *Which one* would you ("mother") like?

> **Ini?** *This one?*

> *Bukan,* **itu.** No, *that one.*

Yang is also used to introduce subordinate clauses, just like the English word "which."

> *Kain batik* **yang** *kita beli sudah luntur.*
> The batik cloth *which* we bought has lost its color.

> *Film* **yang** *kita lihat itu bagus sekali!*
> That film *which* we saw was very good!

PART THREE

Small Talk

Indonesians are great talkers. They are also an instinctively inquisitive people, and will often approach you on buses or trains to strike up a conversation. As expressed in the common greetings *Mau ke mana?* and *Sudah makan belum?* they always seem to want to know where you are going, what you are doing, who you are, whether you have eaten or bathed yet, etc. Just as we automatically say "How are you?" or "How do you do?" in English when meeting someone, these greetings do not require a specific answer, but are simply another way of saying hello.

Once the greetings are over, however, visitors will frequently find themselves barraged with a series of more specific questions, including many that seem to concern very personal and intimate matters, such as family background, marital status, religious beliefs, and so forth. These will come up again and again until you can almost predict which question is coming next, and are probably quite tired of this whole "interview" process.

Try not be put off by this. Understand that your "interviewers" are simply trying to be friendly, and are using such topics to make small talk, much as Westerners would discuss the weather or sports. Realize that in Indonesia such information is not considered personal at all, it is simply a part of one's identity—like your name, nationality and address. If you do not wish to answer, it is perfectly acceptable to be evasive or to joke around. Most Indonesians will never press you for an answer. On the other hand, you can use this as an opportunity to practice your Indonesian, and by turning the questions around you can also interact with and learn something about the people you meet.

The following sections will equip you with basic phrases and vocabulary to deal with these "20 questions" that you will encounter again and again when traveling in Indonesia.

Name and Nationality

One of the first questions asked, following your name, will be about your nationality.

Nama bapak/ibu siapa? or *Siapa nama bapak/ibu?*
What is your name?

Siapa namanya? What is your name?

Nama saya Martin. My name is Martin.

Nama saya Jane. My name is Jane.

Bapak/Ibu asal dari mana?
   or
Asal bapak/ibu dari mana? } Where do you come from?
   or
Asalnya dari mana?

Saya dari Amérika.	I am from America.
or *Saya orang Amérika.*	I am American.
Australia	Australian
Belanda	Dutch
Dénmark	Danish
Inggris	British
Italia	Italian
Jepang	Japanese
Jérman	German
Kanada	Canadian
Thailand	Thai
Norwégia	Norwegian
Perancis	French
Selandia Baru	New Zealander
Spanyol	Spanish
Swédia	Swedish
Swis	Swiss
Tionghoa, Cina	Chinese
Yunani	Greek

Note: *Inggris* alone or *negara Inggris* means the country, England (or Great Britain), *orang Inggris* is a Briton and *babasa Inggris* is the English language. Similarly, *Jérman* or *negara Jérman* is Germany, *orang Jerman* is a German person and *bahasa Jérman* is the language. So it is with other countries, nationalities and languages.

Amérika   Jepang   Jérman

Age

3.02

The next thing most people want to know is your age.

umur age	**berumur** to be of the age, have the age ...
tahun year(s)	**lahir** to be born
muda young	**tua** old

Umur bapak/ibu berapa (tahun)? How old are you?

Umurnya berapa (tahun)? How old are you?
(lit: "Your age is how many [years]?")

Umur saya empat puluh satu (tahun). I am 41 (years old).
(lit: "My age is 41.")

Saya berumur tiga puluh tahun. I am 30 years old.

Saya lahir tahun sembilan belas enam puluh satu.
I was born in 1961.

In answering evasively, you may want to joke and say:

Saya sudah tua, mau pénsiun. I am already old, ready to retire.

Saya masih muda. I am still young.

Family

3.03

Next you will be asked about your family and marital status. Indonesians expect all adults over 25 to be married and all married couples to have children, and will be surprised if they find this is not the case. If you are over 25 and still single, and don't wish to pursue the matter further, you might consider just saying that you are married and have three children anyway (which is an acceptable answer).

De facto and same-sex partners are not openly recognized in Indonesian culture, so it is better to refer to them as your husband or wife. Divorce also carries a social stigma, so avoid mentioning this unless you know the person well.

ayah, bapak father	***ibu*** mother
isteri wife	***suami*** husband
perempuan woman, female	***laki-laki*** male, man
kawin, nikah to be married	***keluarga*** family

saudara brother or sister (sibling)

adik younger sibling	***kakak*** older sibling
pacar boy- or girlfriend	***ternan, kawan*** friend

anak child   *orang* person
anak perempuan daughter   *anak laki-laki* son
cucu grandchild, great-niece or -nephew
orang tua parents (lit: "old people")

Bapak/Ibu sudah kawin belum? Are you married yet?

Sudah/Belum. Already/Not yet.

Masih muda. (I am) still too young.

Anaknya berapa? How many children do you have?

Tiga. Three.

Satu laki-laki dan dua perempuan.
One son and two daughters.

Berapa bersaudara?
How many brothers and sisters do you have?

Saya tiga bersaudara. I have three siblings.

Kakak laki-laki satu dan adik perempuan duo.
One older brother and two younger sisters.

3.04

Additional vocabulary

bayi baby   *bibi* aunt
cerai divorced (avoid saying this where possible)
ipar brother/sister-in-law
kakék grandfather, grand uncle
keponakan niece or nephew
menantu son/daughter-in-law
mertua father/mother-in-law
nénék grandmother, great-aunt
paman uncle   *(saudara) sepupu* cousin

Occupation

3.05

Next will be questions concerning your job or profession. Most educated Indonesians carry a business card. They may offer you one and ask for yours. After even a brief conversation, many people will want to have your address. This may just be a source of pride for them, but exchanging name cards may come in useful. If you will be traveling for very long in Indonesia, it is a good idea to have some cards printed. This can be done cheaply and quickly in any town, and saves you from having to write out your name and address.

bekerja to work	*pénsion* retired
perusahaan company	*belajar* to study
kartu card	*kartu nama* name card

Bapak/Ibu kerja di mana? Where do you work?

Saya bekerja di perusahaan... I work at a ... company

Saya bekerja di kantor. I work in an office.

Saya kuliah. I am studying at university.

Saya kena PHK (pé ha ka).
I am unemployed.

Ada kartu nama?
Do you have a name card?

Boléh saya minta satu?
May I have one?

Maaf, tidak ada.
I'm sorry I don't have one.

3.06

Additional vocabulary

ilmuwan scientist

karyawan/-wati white collar worker (m/f)

mahasiswa/mahasiswi university student (m/f)

olahragawan/-wati athlete (m/f)

wartawan/-wati journalist (m/f)

dosén university lecturer   *guru* teacher

manajer manager   *misionaris* missionary

pengusaha businessman   *pengarang* writer

pegawai negeri civil servant   *pelaut* sailor

sékrétaris secretary   *seniman* artist

3.07

Religion

It is common for Indonesians to ask about your religion. For most people in Indonesia, religion is not so much a question of personal beliefs as it is a reflection of one's ethnic or cultural identity. There are now six recognized religions: Buddhism, Hinduism, Islam, Confucianism, Catholicism and Protestantism. The last two are considered to be separate religions in their own right, and Indonesians will expect most Westerners to follow one of them. Atheism is not officially recognized, and it is not a good idea to say you are atheist, as this suggests links to discredited communist groups in the 1960s. To Indonesians, it is like not having a name or a nationality. When in doubt, just say that you are *Kristen* or *Katolik*. If you are lapsed, you can add *KTP* (*ka té pé*) after your religion, meaning that you are only an adherent in name (eg. *Kristen KTP*).

agama religion	***anggota*** member
geréja church	***masuk*** enter, convert

Bapak/Ibu agama apa? What religion are you?

Saya orang Hindu. I am Hindu.

Banyak orang Bali begitu. So are many Balinese.

Saya orang Islam. I am a Muslim.

Katolik Catholic	*Budha* Buddhist
Kristen Protestant	*Yahudi* Jewish

Note: As a result of Dutch influence, Indonesians make a clear distinction between Protestants and Catholics, and have no general term to express "Christian." To say that one is *Kristen* in Indonesian means specifically that one is Protestant. Note also that in certain areas of Indonesia, where Islam is particularly strong, it may not be a good idea to say that you are Jewish, although in most places this will not create any problems.

Weather

The weather in Indonesia is hot and humid all year around, so there is not much to talk about. One thing that people do often talk about, however, are the rains and great floods or *banjir* that periodically inundate cities and towns during the rainy season. People may also ask you how the weather is back home.

In the southernmost chain of islands (Java, Bali and Nusa Tenggara to the east), there are two seasons: a rainy season (from about September to March) and a dry one (April to August). On the other islands, closer to the equator, the rainfall is more evenly spread throughout the year, though certain months have more rain than others.

banjir flood, flooding	*hujan* rain, to be raining
derajat degrees	*cuaca* weather
matahari sun	*salju* snow
sering often, frequent[ly]	*suhu* temperature

panas hot   *dingin* cold
cerah clear   *sejuk* cool
mendung, berawan cloudy, overcast
segar fresh, invigorating

musim season   *iklim* climate
musim panas summer (*panas* = "hot")
musim gugur fall (*gugur* = "to fall")
musim dingin winter (*dingin* = "cold")
musim semi spring (*semi* = "to sprout")
musim kemarau dry season
musim hujan rainy season, monsoon

(Cuacanya) panas hari ini. The weather is hot today.

Suhunya tiga puluh derajat. It's 30 degrees (Celsius).

Musim hujan sudah mulai belum?
Have the rains begun yet?

Ya, sudah musim hujan sekarang.
Yes, it is [already] the rainy season now.

Tiap hari hujan. It rains every day.

Tahun ini sering banjir.
This year there has been frequent flooding.

Cuaca di negeri anda bagaimana?
How is the weather in your country?

Sekarang dingin sekali. Ada salju.
It is very cold now. There is snow.

Time

3.09

Time

menit minute	*jam* hour, o'clock
hari day	*minggu* week
bulan month; moon	*tahun* year
hari ini today	*kemarin* yesterday
bésok tomorrow	*lusa* the day after tomorrow
awal early	*terlambat* late
sebelum before	*sesudah* after

sekarang now   *segera* soon

dulu before, earlier, first, beforehand

baru, baru tadi just, just now

nanti later   *sebentar* in a moment, a while

jarang rarely   *kadang-kadang* sometimes

sering often

Kapan mau berangkat? When do you want to depart?

Kita mau pergi hari ini. We want to go today.

Kita mau berangkat pagi. We want to leave early.

Keréta api itu selalu terlambat! That train is always late!

Kemarin terlambat dua jam. Yesterday it was two hours late.

Sering datang ke Indonesia?
Have you often been to Indonesia?

Jarang. Dulu pernah datang sekali.
Rarely. I have come once before.

Kapan tiba di sini? When did you arrive here?

Baru kemarin. Just yesterday.

Kapan berangkat? When are you leaving?

Sebentar lagi. In a little while.

Telling time

3.10

Jam berapa sekarang? What time is it now?

Sekarang jam sepuluh. It is now ten o'clock.

Just as in English, there are several ways of telling the time in Indonesian. One can say "a quarter to nine" or "eight forty-five" or "forty-five minutes past eight."

Jam dua belas seperempat. 12:15

Jam dua belas léwat seperempat. 12:15

Jam dua belas léwat lima belas (menit). 12:15

Note that Indonesians follow the Dutch (European) system in telling time, in which the half hour is normally counted before, not after the hour of day:

Jam setengah sebelas. Half past ten (i.e. 10:30).

To express minutes after the hour, the words *léwat* or *lebih* meaning "past" may be used, although these are optional.

Jam dua léwat *empat puluh lima menit.* 2:45
Jam lima lebih *dua puluh menit.* 5:20

The use of *menit* is also optional, as it is easily understood from the context.

Jam empat kurang sepuluh (menit). 3:50 pm

To express minutes before the hour, the word *kurang* "less" must be used.

Jam tiga kurang seperempat. 2:45

"Half" and "quarter" are used just as in English.

 Note: If a number precedes the word *jam*, it signifies a number of hours; if it follows, it signifies the time of day (= o'clock).

> *dua jam* two hours   *jam dua* two o'clock

Dari Denpasar ke Ubud berapa jam?
How many hours [does it take] to go from Denpasar to Ubud?

Satu jam. One hour.

Berapa jam ke Jakarta? How many hours to Jakarta?

Tiga jam setengah. Three and a half hours.

Periods of the day

In English we break the day into morning, noon, afternoon, evening and night. Indonesians break up the day a bit differently (the following are approximate times).

pagi morning (7 to 11 am; strictly, 0:00 to 10:30–11 am)

siang midday (11 am to 3 pm)

soré late afternoon to dusk (3 to 7 pm)

malam night (7 to 10 pm)

Note that these periods of the day are used not only in greetings with *selamat* (see Part One: Greetings) but also in place of our *am* or *pm* in telling time.

jam sembilan pagi 9 am

jam sembilan malam 9 pm

jam dua siang 2 pm

jam lima soré 5 pm

jam lima pagi 5 am

Doubling Indonesian words signifying periods of the day intensifies their meaning.

pagi-pagi early morning (5 to 7 am)

malam-malam late night (10–12 pm)

tengah malam midnight to sunrise

Used alone, these words can mean "early" or "late," depending on what time of day it is.

Masih pagi. It's still early.

Terlalu soré. Too late (said in middle of the day)

Days of the week

3.12

hari day	*(hari) Minggu* Sunday
(hari) Senin Monday	*(hari) Selasa* Tuesday
(hari) Rabu Wednesday	*(hari) Kamis* Thursday
(hari) Jumat Friday	*(hari) Sabtu* Saturday

Ini hari apa? What day (of the week) is it?

Ini hari Selasa. It is Tuesday.

Dates

tanggal date (of the month)

Januari	January	*Juli*	July
Fébruari	February	*Agustus*	August
Maret	March	*Séptémber*	September
April	April	*Oktober*	October
Méi	May	*Nopember*	November
Juni	June	*Désémber*	December

Hari ini tanggal berapa? What is the date today?

Lahir tahun berapa? What year were you born in?

Saya lahir tangg al duabelas (bulan) Juli tahun (sembilan belas) sembilan puluh satu.
I was born on the twelfth of (the month of) July, the year 1991.

Tahun dua ribu sebelas The year 2011

Saya mau pulang tanggal sepuluh.
I want to go back on the tenth.

Useful words and phrases

lalu, yang lalu past, last
minggu (yang) lalu last week
bulan (yang) lalu last month
tahun (yang) lalu last year
sejak since

Sejak kapan? Since when? For how long?
Sejak tahun lalu. Since last year.

depan next, front
minggu depan next week
bulan depan next month
tahun depan next year

tadi a while ago
tadi pagi earlier this morning
tadi malam, semalam last night
tadi siang earlier today (midday)
tadi soré earlier this afternoon

nanti later
nanti siang later today (midday)
nanti soré later this afternoon
nanti malam later tonight

 Note: When *malam* (night, eve) precedes a day of the week, it indicates the night before that day (i.e. the eve of that day). When in doubt, it is best to state the date when fixing an appointment in order to remove any ambiguity.

malam Sabtu Saturday eve (= Friday night)
Sabtu malam Saturday night
tanggal dua belas the twelfth

PART FOUR

Getting Around

4.01

Asking Directions

alamat address	*alun-alun* town square
désa village, countryside	*gedung* building
kota city, town, downtown	*rumah* house/home
pompa bénsin gas station	*tempat* place
gang alleyway, lane	*jalan* street
jalan kecil side street	*jalan besar* main street
jalan raya highway, thoroughfare	*jalan tol* expressway, tollroad
léwat pass, go by way of	*bélok* to turn
kanan right	*kiri* left
terus straight	*kira-kira* approximately

Indonesians are more than willing to give you directions if they can understand what you are asking them. Note that since the place you are asking about is invariably the main topic of your question, you should always place it at or near the beginning of your sentence (not at the end, as in English). This will make your question more easily understood. It is also more polite to preface any request for directions by the phrase **Mau tanya** (lit: "Want ask"), or **Saya mau tanya** ("I want to ask").

Mau tanya. Excuse me, I wish to ask.

Hotel Savoy Homann di mana?
Where is the Hotel Savoy Homann?

Jalan Sudirman di mana? Where is Jalan Sudirman?

Gedung Nusantara di mana? Where is the Nusantara Building?

Ke Ubud léwat mana? How do you get to Ubud?

Ke Yogya naik apa dari sini? How can I get to Jogja from here?
(i.e. by what means of transportation?)

Terus saja di sini, lalu bélok kanan.
Straight ahead here, then turn right.

Léwat jalan ini terus, sampai jalan raya.
Follow this road straight until the highway.

Lalu bélok kiri. Then turn left.

Berapa jauh (dari sini)? How far is it from here?

Kira-kira lima kilométer. About five kilometers.

 Note: When asking directions, phrase your question in such a way that it cannot be answered by a simple yes or no. For example, don't say: "Is Jalan Malioboro over there?" The person being asked may not understand what you are saying and may simply respond yes or no at random. Instead, ask: "Where is Jalan Malioboro?"

 ## Taxi directions

4.02 The following are indispensible phrases for dealing with taxi drivers:

Tolong panggil taksi! Please summon a taxi!

Saya mau ke... I want to go to...

Ke bandara, pak. To the airport, *pak.*

Mau léwat mana? By which route?

Yang paling cepat. The fastest one.

Saya mau léwat... I want to go by way of...

Terus! or **Lurus!** Straight ahead!

Bélok kiri/kanan. Turn left/right.

Stop! or **Berhenti!** Stop!

Di sini! Here!

Putar! Turn around/make a U-turn.

Mundur! Back up!

Pelan-pelan! Slowly!

Cepat! Faster! Quickly!

Awas! or **Hati-hati!** Be careful!

Ini ke arah utara? Is this to the north?

selatan?	south?
timur?	east?
barat?	west?

Public Transportation

4.03

pergi go	*balik, kembali* return
berangkat depart	*datang, tiba* arrive
batal cancel	*tunda* postpone

naik ride, go by (train, bus, etc.)

pulang go back (home)

sampai reach, until

jadwal schedule

kantor office

karcis, tiket ticket

tempat duduk seat

sopir driver

ongkos fare, rate

setasiun (keréta api) train station

términal (bis) bus terminal

belum not yet	*langsung* direct, non-stop
masih still, left over	*sudah* already
lambat slow	*cepat* fast

Once again, when asking a question, state the main topic first so that the person being asked knows what it is you are referring to.

Términal bis di mana? Where is the bus terminal?

Setasiun keréta api di mana? Where is the train station?

Ke bandara berapa kilométer dari sini?
How many kilometers to the airport from here?

Ongkosnya berapa? What is the fare?

Ke Bali bisa naik keréta api tidak?
Can I take a train to Bali or not?

Keréta api ke Yogya berangkat jam berapa?
What time does the train to Jogja depart?

Pesawat ke Jakarta tiba jam berapa?
What time does the plane to Jakarta arrive?

Ke Bali hari ini ada bis lagi tidak?
Is there another bus to Bali today or not?

Masih ada tempat duduk? Are there any seats left?

Masih. Yes, there are still.

Maaf, sudah habis. Sorry, sold out (finished) already.

Berapa harga karcisnya? What is the price of the tickets?

Sekali jalan atau pulang pergi? One-way or round-trip?

Sekali jalan. One way.

Ongkosnya lima belas ribu rupiah. The fare is Rp. 15.000.

Naik bis ke Médan berapa jam, pak?
How many hours by bus to Medan, *pak*?

Biasanya lima belas jam. Usually 15 hours.

Bis ini lambat atau cepat? Is this bus slow or fast?

Ada bis éksprés? Is there an express bus?

Berangkat jam berapa? What time does it leave?

Pakai AC ("ah-say") tidak?
Does it have air-conditioning or not?

Bis ke Solo itu léwat mana?
What route does the bus to Solo follow?

Sampai di Malang jam berapa?
What time does it reach Malang?

Paling cepat naik apa? What is the fastest way?

Taruh bagasi di mana? Where do I put my baggage?

Séwa mobil ini berapa per hari?
How much does it cost to rent this car per day?

Pakai sopir tidak? Do you want it with the driver?

Tidak. Saya mau setir sendiri. No. I want to drive myself.

Saya punya SIM intérnasional.
I have an international driver's license.

Modes of transportation

4.04

Saya mau naik... I want to go by...

   pesawat (terbang) airplane

   kapal ship

   perahu boat

   keréta api train

   mobil car/automobile

   bis (malam) (night) bus

   travel door-to-door minibus service

   taksi taxi

   angkot minibus

   colt (pronounced *kol*) minivan

   bémo small pick-up or minivan

   bajaj (pronounced *bajai*) three-wheeled minicar

   dokar horse and cart   **kuda** horse

   bécak pédicab   **tukang bécak** pedicab driver

   sepéda bicycle

   (sepéda) motor motorcycle

Accommodation

4.05

Accommodation in Indonesia is generally good value for money. It ranges from luxury suites costing hundreds of dollars a night to inexpensive rooms in lodges called *losmén*. Ask the price of a room first, and have a look before checking in. You will have to fill out a registration form and may be asked to pay in advance. Discounts can often be had for the asking. If you are paying extra for air-conditioning, make sure it works before paying.

Indonesians now use the words *cékin* and *cékout*. Checkout time is normally 12 noon and you may be charged for another night if you stay beyond that. Many Indonesians you meet will invite you to stay in their home, and good friends may be offended (or will at least act so) if you pay a visit without spending the night.

hotél hotel	*losmén* small, cheap hotel
penginapan small hotel (cheap)	
wisma guesthouse (medium-priced)	
kamar room	*kunci* key
bagasi baggage	*koper* suitcase
bon bill	*tarip* rate, tariff
penuh full	*kosong* empty, vacant

daftar register   *titip* leave with someone
cékin check in   *cékout* check out
cuci wash   *bersihkan* clean

Masih ada kamar? Are there still rooms available?

Masih. Yes, there still are.

Untuk berapa orang? For how many people?

Untuk tiga orang. For three people.

Maaf, sudah penuh. I'm sorry, we are already full.

Berapa per malam? What (how much) is the rate per night?

Ada kamar yang lebih murah? Do you have cheaper rooms?

Boléh saya lihat kamar dulu?
May I see the room first?

Ini kuncinya.
Here is the key.

Berapa malam tinggal di sini?
How many nights will you stay, sir/ma'am?

Tiga malam. Three nights.

Silakan isi dulu. Please register first.

Ini kuncinya. Here is the key.

Kuncinya dititip di depan kalau keluar.
Please leave the key at reception if you go out.

Saya mau bayar sekarang. I want to pay the bill now.

Mas! Tolong ambil bagasi. Porter! Please take our luggage.

Minta air minum. Please give us some drinking water.

Ada banyak nyamuk. There are lots of mosquitoes.

Kamarnya tolong disemprot. Please spray the room.

Tolong bersihkan kamar sekarang.
Please clean/make up the room now.

Tolong cuci pakaian ini. Please wash these clothes.

Note: Boiled water for drinking is normally supplied in a thermos or in a bottle, and you should never drink water from the tap. A tip of Rp. 1.000 (small hotels) to Rp. 5.000 (larger hotels) will be appreciated by a porter or room boy, depending on the service rendered.

Useful vocabulary

A/C (pronounced *ah-say*) air-conditioning
kipas angin electric fan

bantal pillow	*kelambu* mosquito netting
handuk towel	*kasur* mattress
selimut blanket	*seperéi* bedsheet
guling bolster pillow (Dutch wife)	

air panas hot water	*gayung* water ladle, dipper
kamar mandi bathroom	*mandi* wash, bathe
gosok iron; scrub	*toalét, klosét* toilet

kursi chair	*lampu* light
méja table	*tempat tidur* bed

Note: Bathrooms in cheap hotels do not have bathtubs or showers, just a tub of cold water (*bak mandi*) and a ladle (*gayung*). You are not supposed to climb into the tub, but should instead use the ladle to splash water over yourself while standing outside it ("slosh and wash"). Some smaller hotels also do not have flush toilets, and you have to use the ladle to flush water down the toilet after use.

Sightseeing

4.07 Buddhist and Hindu temples, palaces and religious monuments are some of the hottest attractions in Indonesia. In Java, you should not miss the *kraton* or palaces of Jogja, Solo and Cirebon, or the *wayang kulit* and *wayang wong* puppet and dance performances. In Bali, there are many lovely temples as well as numerous dance performances and temple festivals. On these and other islands you will also find beautiful volcanic scenery and sculpted rice terraces.

kunjungi, mengunjungi to visit

nonton, menonton to watch, observe (a show, film)

obyék wisata tourist attraction

turis (foreign) tourist   *wisatawan* tourist

pariwisata tourism

air terjun waterfall   *cagar alam* nature reserve

danau lake   *telaga* lake

pulau island	*gua* cave
gunung mountain	*gunung api* volcano
hutan forest, jungle	*mata air panas* hot spring
pemandangan panorama, view	

candi ancient temple (Hindu or Buddhist)

bénténg fortress	*kraton* palace
kebun binatang zoo	*klénténg* Chinese temple
mesjid mosque	*musium* museum
patung statue	*taman* garden, park
puri Balinese palace	*pura* Balinese Hindu temple

makam, kuburan gravesite

menara tower, lighthouse

peninggalan kuno archeological remains

geréja church	*kuil* temple

pertunjukan performance	*tarian* dance

wayang kulit shadow puppet show

wayang wong traditional Javanese theater

Mau kunjungi candi Borobudur hari ini?
Do you want to visit Borobudur temple today?

Tidak. Saya mau ke kraton dulu.
No. I want to go to the palace first.

Ayo kita nonton tarian. Let's watch a dance.

Jam berapa ada pertunjukan? What time is the performance?

Di Pangandaran ada cagar alam.
At Pangandaran there is a nature reserve.

Ada kebun binatang di sini? Tidak. Is there a zoo here? No.

4.08

Leisure Activities

baca (buku) to read (books)

berjalan, jalan-jalan to walk, go walking

main play   *renang* swim

tidur sleep   *télevisi* television

badminton, bulu tangkis badminton

bioskop movie theater, cinema

kolam renang swimming pool

lapangan field, court

lapangan ténis tennis court

ténis tennis

sépak bola football (soccer)

pantai beach

pasir sand

Saya mau berenang di pantai.
I am going swimming at the beach.

Anda mau ikut tidak? Would you like to come along?

Tidak, saya mau baca buku. No, I want to read a book.

Ada lapangan ténis di sini? Are there tennis courts here?

Buka jam berapa? What time do they open?

Mari kita ke kolam renang. Let's go to the swimming pool.

Mari kita nonton di bioskop. Let's go to the cinema.

Apakah ada bioskop dekat sini? Is there a cinema near here?

Ada film apa malam ini? What film is playing tonight?

Travel Tips

Getting around Indonesia is easy and inexpensive, if often somewhat slow and uncomfortable with all the heat, dust, smoke and crowds. Allow plenty of time to get to where you are going, and always expect some delays!

As Indonesians are doing constantly, it is a good idea to ask as many questions (of as many different people) as possible about the destination of a particular bus or train, what time it departs, whether it is late, the route, how long it will take to get there, how much it costs, and so forth. You will find that you receive a wide variety of answers, and by asking a number of times of various people you will (hopefully) get a good idea of what to expect.

Many local forms of transportation like buses, minibuses and pedicabs have no posted prices. It is best to ask a disinterested party the approximate price for transportation before you depart, or try to see what others are paying. Always have small change handy, and offer what you think is the correct amount to the conductor. He will tell you if it is not enough.

If you and your party are the only passengers in a car, pedicab or minibus, you must bargain and fix a price *before you depart*. State clearly where you are going, and ask the price. The driver may try to wave you into the vehicle, but a price must be agreed upon first or you may end up paying more than you expected later. If you are not sure, ask in your hotel beforehand how much the fare should be.

When bargaining, offer what you feel is a fair amount and then walk away slowly, repeating the amount several times in a friendly way. The driver will usually call you back. In the end, you should expect to pay a bit more because you are a foreigner. And don't expect to get change back from big bank notes!

PART FIVE

Eating and Drinking

5.01

Dining in Indonesia can be an extraordinarily pleasurable experience, particularly if you are adventuresome enough to sample the local cuisine. The following basic words and phrases are designed to help you read menus and order food in Indonesian restaurants.

rumah makan small, simple restaurant

réstoran (classier) restaurant

warung roadside stall

makan eat	*makanan* food
masak cook	*masakan* cooking, cuisine
minum drink	*minuman* a drink , drinks

sarapan breakfast

makan siang lunch (lit: "midday meal")

makan malam dinner (lit: "evening meal")

dingin cold	*panas* hot (temperature)
pesan order	*lagi* more
bon bill	*daftar makanan, ménu* menu
daftar minuman drinks menu	

Mas! Waiter! (used in Java, Bali)

Mbak! Waitress! (used in Java, Bali)

Kak! Waitress! (used in Sumatra)

pisau knife   *garpu* fork

séndok spoon   *piring* plate

gelas glass   *mangkok* bowl

cangkir cup   *sumpit* chopsticks

tisu paper napkins

Ada masakan Indonesia di sini?
Do you have Indonesian food here?

Boléh lihat ménu/daftar makanan? May [I, we] see the menu?

Saya mau pesan... I would like to order...

satu porsi... one portion ...

setengah porsi... half a portion ...

Minta garpu dan séndok. Please give me a fork and spoon.

Minta satu lagi. I would like one more.

Ada minuman dingin (dari kulkas)?
Do you have cold drinks (from the refrigerator)?

Minta satu botol bir dingin. Give me one bottle of cold beer.

Tidak pakai és. I don't want ice. (lit: "Not with ice.")

Minta gelas kosong. I would like an empty glass.

Minta bon. I would like the bill.

Note: When eating informally at home, Indonesians may use the fingers of the right hand without any utensils. You will see people eating this way in roadside stalls or *warung*, sometimes in small restaurants as well. When eating out in classier restaurants, however, forks and spoons are more commonly used. Table knives are found only in Western restaurants serving dishes like steak which require cutting, while chopsticks are provided only in Chinese restaurants.

Basic Food Terms

5.02

air (pron: "AYE-er") water	*nasi* cooked rice
air minum drinking water	*gula* sugar
kéju cheese	*kuah* broth, soup
tahu soybean curd, tofu	*roti* bread
témpé soybean cakes	*telur* egg

mie wheat noodles (usually made with egg)

bihun rice vermicelli   *kué* cake, cookie

Note: Most meals in Indonesia center around rice as the staple. The phrase *makan nasi* "eating rice" is in fact often used to mean eating in general. Anything without rice is only considered a snack or a light meal. Noodles are a common light lunch or snack and are widely available, especially in Chinese restaurants. *Tahu* and *témpé* are inexpensive meat substitutes made from soybeans. They are now quite popular in the West, especially among vegetarians, because they are high in protein yet low in fat and cholesterol.

5.03

Vegetables *Sayuran*

bawang onion   *bawang putih* garlic

bayam spinach   *buncis* green beans

caisim, bok coy Chinese cabbage

jagung corn   *jamur* mushrooms, fungus

kacang beans, nuts   *kacang panjang* long beans

kentang potatoes   *kangkung* water spinach

kacang kapri snowpeas   *kol* cabbage

sawi Chinese cabbage   *selada* lettuce

seledri celery   *timun* cucumber

tanpa daging without meat, vegetarian

térong eggplant, aubergine

tomat tomato   *wortel* carrot

Be careful if you are vegetarian. *Tanpa daging* is often understood to mean "without red meat," and you may end up with food containing chicken or seafood. It is probably better to ask for *sayur saja* (lit. "just vegetables").

Meat *Daging*

ayam chicken

bébék duck

kambing mutton

bakso meatballs (usually beef)

buntut oxtail

saté satay, grilled meat on skewers

babi pork

sapi beef

hati liver

babat tripe

Seafood *Seafood*

cumi-cumi, sotong cuttlefish, squid

ikan fish

kepiting crab

udang shrimp, prawn

udang besar lobster

tiram oysters

Cooking Terms

bakar grilled, toasted

goréng fry, fried

rebus boil, boiled

kering dry

matang well-cooked, ripe, well-done

mentah raw, uncooked, rare

bubur porridge (usually rice, with meat added)

sop clear soup

soto spicy soup (with meat)

kukus steamed

panggang roasted

muda unripe, young

basah wet, fresh

Breakfast *Sarapan*

5.07

Breakfast is usually included in the price of a hotel room in Indonesia. For breakfast, many Indonesians eat fried rice (*nasi goréng*) or bread (*roti*) with tea or coffee. In restaurants catering for foreigners, eggs and toast are also served, often with fresh fruits and juices.

> *mentéga* butter
>
> **roti bakar** toast
> (lit: "toasted bread")
>
> *selai* jam
>
> **telur dadar** scrambled egg
>
> **telur goréng** fried egg "over easy"
>
> **telur mata sapi** fried egg "sunny side up"
>
> **telur rebus** hard boiled egg
>
> **telur rebus setengah matang** soft boiled egg

Common Menu Items

5.08

Most lunch and dinner menus are subdivided into sections containing rice and noodle dishes, meat, seafood, vegetables and drinks. If your order is not taken by a waiter or waitress, you will usually be given a pad of paper on which to write down your order. Once you have done this, push it to the end of the table or *wave* it around so the waiter/waitress will come and pick it up.

When you have finished eating, you can ask for the bill by saying **Sudah!** "Already!" or **Minta bon** (asking for the bill). In some restaurants, you have to pay the proprietor at the main counter on the way out.

In most Indonesian restaurants, you will find a fairly "standard" menu containing some or all of the following dishes:

> *ayam goréng* chicken stewed in coconut cream and spices, then deep fried

ayam goréng kecap chicken fried with sweet soy sauce

cap cay goréng stir-fried mixed vegetables (with meat)

cap cay kuah mixed vegetable soup (with meat)

fu yung hai Chinese-style omelette (with onions and meat)

gado-gado mixed vegetables with peanut sauce

gudeg young jackfruit (and sometimes chicken) stewed in coconut cream and spices

gulai kambing spicy curried mutton stew

karé ayam chicken curry

kepiting goréng deep-fried crab

kepiting rebus steamed crab

mie bakso Chinese noodles with meatballs

mie goréng fried noodles with meat and vegetables

mie kuah Chinese noodle soup

mie pangsit dumpling (won ton) noodle soup

nasi campur, nasi rames "mixed rice" (i.e. rice with several side dishes)

nasi goréng fried rice with meat (often with a fried egg)

nasi rawon spicy beef stew with rice

pecel mixed vegetables with spicy peanut sauce

rujak raw vegetable salad with a sweet and spicy sauce

saté ayam chicken satay

saté kambing mutton satay

sayur asam sour vegetable soup (with baby corn, green beans, eggplant, peanuts, jackfruit nuts)

sayur lodéh vegetables stewed in coconut milk

soto ayam spicy chicken soup (with rice or noodles)

udang goréng mentéga prawns stir-fried in butter

udang rebus steamed prawns

Note: To order any of the above vegetable or egg dishes without meat, place the words "without meat" (***tanpa daging***) after the name of the dish. For example: ***cap cay goréng tanpa daging*** ("stir-fried mixed vegetables without meat"). If you would like the dish not too spicy, you should add the words ***tidak pedas*** ("not spicy") or ***tidak pakai cabé*** ("don't use chili").

 5.09

Condiments and Snacks

acar pickles	***permén*** candy
garam salt	***gula*** sugar
jahé ginger	***madu*** honey
merica, lada pepper	***cabé, lombok*** chili pepper

emping fried crackers made of melinjo nuts

krupuk prawn (or fish) crackers

kécap (manis) (sweet) soy sauce

kacang nuts, beans	***saus kacang*** peanut sauce
sambal chili sauce	***saus tomat*** tomato sauce

sambal terasi chili sauce with fermented prawn paste

 Notes: The most common condiments found in Indonesian restaurants are pickles (*acar*), sweet soy sauce (*kécap manis*) and some form of chili sauce (*sambal*). You will also find large containers filled with various types of fried wafers, crackers and cracklings (*krupuk*). You may help yourself to the latter, and the waiter will add them to your bill.

Fruits *Buah*

anggur grape   *apel* apple

strobéri strawberry   *belimbing* starfruit, carambola

durian durian   *jeruk* orange, citrus

jeruk bali pomelo (pink grapefruit)

jeruk nipis, limau lemon

kelapa coconut   *mangga* mango

nanas pineapple   *nangka* jackfruit

papaya papaya   *pisang* banana

rambutan small, hairy red fruit, like a lychee

semangka watermelon

salak "snakeskin fruit" with white apple-like flesh inside

Note: The variety of fruits in Indonesia is astounding. Some, like durians and mangos, are seasonal. Many others, like bananas, papayas and pineapples, are available all year round. It is fun to poke around in the markets, and also cheaper to buy your fruit there.

Drinks *Minuman*

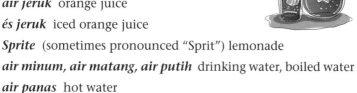

air botol, aqua bottled water

air és iced water

air jeruk orange juice

és jeruk iced orange juice

Sprite (sometimes pronounced "Sprit") lemonade

air minum, air matang, air putih drinking water, boiled water

air panas hot water

jus juice   *és* ice

anggur wine   *bir* beer

kopi coffee (black with sugar)
kopi pahit black coffee without sugar
kopi susu coffee with milk and sugar
kopi susu tanpa gula coffee with milk only

susu milk
susu panas hot sweetened milk
susu coklat panas hot chocolate

és téh (manis) ice (sweet) tea
téh panas hot tea
téh botol bottled tea
téh pahit, téh tawar, téh tong (Sumatra) hot tea with no sugar

kopyor coconut milk
kelapa muda iced young coconut milk

Lots of drinks, including most soft drinks, are known by their brand names. These include Coca Cola, 7 Up, Sprite ("sprit"), Fanta, Milo, Ovaltine, and so forth.

Most Indonesian drinks—including coffee, tea and fruit juices—come heavily sweetened with sugar. If you want them without sugar, or with only a little sugar, you have to specify this when you order. Coffee and tea are normally served sweet but without milk, so if you want milk you have to add the word *susu*. Finally, you need to specify if you want the drink hot or cold.

pahit bitter
téh pahit black tea without sugar
téh susu panas hot tea with milk and sugar
tanpa gula without sugar
kopi tanpa gula black coffee without sugar
kopi susu tanpa gula coffee with milk but no sugar
és kopi iced black coffee with sugar

sedikit gula a little sugar only

és jeruk dengan sedikit gula iced orange juice with only a
   little sugar

Taste

5.12

asam sour

manis sweet

pedas hot (spicy)

asin salty

pahit bitter

énak tasty, nice (lit. delicious)

lumayan quite good, so-so

sedap yummy, delicious

kurang énak not so tasty

rasa feel, taste

segar fresh

Suka masakan Indonesia?
Do you like Indonesian food?

Ya, énak sekali. Yes, it is very nice.

Tidak terlalu pedas?
It's not too hot for you?

Ya, sedikit pedas tapi énak.
Yes, a bit hot, but tasty.

Masakan di réstoran ini kurang énak.
The food at this restaurant is not so tasty.

Ya, ayamnya terlalu asin.
Yes, the chicken is too salty.

Dan sopnya asam sekali.
And the soup is very sour.

Tapi nasi goréngnya sedap!
But the fried rice is delicious!

Notes on Hygiene

It is important to take certain precautions so that your visit to Indonesia will not be marred by serious stomach problems. Intermittent bouts of indigestion or mild diarrhoea are to be expected, as your stomach adjusts to new foods and stray bacteria. More serious, however, are intestinal parasites that can be picked up from food and utensils that are not hygienically handled. The following are a few tips.

Eat in restaurants rather than in *warungs* or roadside stalls. The problem with the latter is that they have no running water with which to clean dishes and utensils, and often a single bucket of water drawn from a nearby river or canal is used for this purpose throughout the day.

Never drink water straight from the tap. All drinking water (*air minum*) must be boiled. Even in luxury hotels, where the water is treated, it is not safe to drink. A thermos of boiled water or bottles of mineral water (*aqua*) are usually provided by the hotel.

Avoid all uncooked foods, including salads and garnishes, except perhaps in the most expensive Western restaurants. Buy fresh fruits and vegetables in the market and clean and peel them yourself rather than purchasing already peeled fruits and vegetables from vendors.

Drink tea or bottled drinks rather than fresh fruit juices and other prepared cold drinks served in smaller restaurants and by vendors. Bottled water is available everywhere in Indonesia, generically known by the brand name *Aqua*.

Avoid ice altogether, as it is sometimes made with unboiled water. This is difficult to do on a hot day, but you should be aware that ice is the most common source of stomach ailments among Indonesians and foreigners alike. Instead, ask for refrigerated bottled drinks (*dingin dari kulkas* = "cold from the refrigerator").

Beware of glasses and utensils that are not well-washed. You will always see Indonesians wiping their fork and spoon with a napkin before eating in a restaurant or buffet.

If you do get sick, it is best to eat plain white rice (*nasi putih*) with vegetable soup (*sop sayur*), bread or rice porridge (*bubur*) and to drink plenty of strong, hot black tea (*téh pahit*).

PART SIX

Happy Shopping

6.01

jual sell	*beli* buy
belanja shop	*rugi* lose money
tawar make an offer (of money)	
tawar-menawar to bargain (back and forth)	
ambil take	*kasih* give

barang goods, item	*harga* price
pasar market	*harga pas* fixed price
mahal expensive	*murah* cheap, inexpensive
toko store	*uang* money
tunai cash	

biasa usual, normal	*désain, corak* design, pattern
warna color	*macam* type, kind
istiméwa special, "the best"	

muda young, light (of colors)

tua old, dark (of colors)

sekali very

mutu, kualitas quality

terlalu too, excessive

Aduh! My goodness! (expression of shock, dismay)

Colors *Warna–warni*

6.02

abu-abu gray	*biru* blue
coklat brown	*hijau* green
hitam black	*kuning* yellow
mérah red	*putih* white

The following is a typical shopping scenario, in which a tourist (T) enters a shop and is waited on by a shopkeeper (S).

S: *Boléh saya bantu?* May I help you?
Cari apa? What are you looking for?

T: *Lihat-lihat saja.* Just looking.

T: *Harga ini berapa?* What is the price of this?

S: *Delapan puluh ribu rupiah.* Rp.80.000. (Rp. = rupiah)

T: *Mahal sekali!* Very expensive!

S: *Tidak, tidak mahal.* No, madam. It's not expensive.
Lihat kualitasnya. Look at the quality.

T: *Ya, tapi terlalu mahal.* Yes, but it is too expensive.

S: *Ya, boléh kurang.* Yes, [the price] can be reduced.
Tawar berapa? How much would you offer?

T: *Tiga puluh ribu rupiah boléh?* Is Rp. 30.000 okay?

S: *Tidak, saya rugi.* No, I will lose money.
Lima puluh ribu rupiah saja. Rp. 50.000 only.

F: *Masih terlalu mahal!* Still too expensive!
Empat puluh ribu, itu sudah harga pas.
Rp. 40.000, that is the normal price.

S: *Ya, boléh.* Yes, okay.
Mau ambil yang mana? Which one do you want to take?

F: *Saya mau ini/ itu.* I want this one/that one.
Ada warna yang lain? Do you have another color?

S: *Ada warna mérah, kuning dan hijau.*
     Yes, I have red, yellow and green.

T: *Saya ambil dua.* Give me two.
     Satu mérah, satu kuning. One red and one yellow.

Bargaining

Bargaining is an essential skill in Indonesia. While in shopping malls and department stores, fixed prices are the norm, in many shops no fixed prices are posted, and it is assumed that bargaining is the rule. This is true in markets and most small shops, as well as for most services. The degree of bargaining required, and the difference between prices normally asked and prices paid, can vary widely.

As a general rule, most Indonesians will never settle for less than a 10% reduction from an asking price. In many cases, however, the asking price may be several times what one normally expects to pay in the end. It simply depends on the situation.

The only places where you don't bargain are in large department stores, supermarkets, restaurants and other establishments that clearly display prices. Even then, however, bargaining for large, costly items can often result in lower prices. (People don't usually bargain over very small amounts, except in the market.)

Be especially wary in souvenir and art shops catering for the tourist trade. Here, it is standard practice to mark up astronomically (often five to ten times the normal price), so as to be able to offer huge discounts to unsuspecting tourists, many of whom are then fooled into thinking that they are getting a great deal.

In order to bargain successfully it is essential to first get a rough idea of the "right price." The best way to find out is to ask an Indonesian or to shop around. In fact, there is no "right price" in any absolute sense, but there is a range of prices that are more or less competitive with what others are charging. Often, as a foreigner, you simply cannot get the lowest prices because you don't have all the bargaining skills at your disposal.

One of the easiest and most straightforward bargaining tactics as a foreigner is to demonstrate right away to the seller that you know roughly what you should pay for an item. You can do this by offering an amount that is 50% to 25% less than the price you expect to pay. The idea is that you start low, the seller starts high, and you then go back and forth several times until you compromise in the middle. Never open with your final offer.

The vendor will feign shock and protest strongly, counteroffering with a much higher price (but less than their first offer). You must also feign shock and protest, offering a bit more than your initial price. This continues until one of you agrees with the other's offer, or until you reach an impasse. When the latter occurs, state your last price several times and begin to walk away slowly. The seller will then accept your price if it is reasonable.

Treat this entire process not as a confrontation, but as a piece of impromptu theater. There are several important things to keep in mind. First of all, never let on how truly interested you are in an item. Point out its many defects, real or imagined. Above all, keep smiling and keep the exchange friendly. By cajoling and bantering good-naturedly with the vendor, you will both have a good time and, equally importantly, you can both maintain your sense of face while arriving at a compromise between your opposing positions.

Some foreigners think they can simply walk into a shop and demand to pay a particular price. This doesn't work. You've got to play the game. Under no circumstances should you get angry because you think the price being asked is too high. Just walk away and shop elsewhere if this is the case.

It is important to understand also that you must follow through on any offer you make, so don't make an offer if you don't intend to buy. You can ask a price out of curiosity, and there is no obligation, but if you make an offer that the seller accepts, you are stuck. Reneging is simply not done in Indonesia, and the seller may rightfully get very angry.

Lastly, be sure that you have agreed on a price before accepting any goods or services. If you simply hop in a pedicab (*bécak*) or a taxi without a meter and tell the driver to take you somewhere without agreeing on a price beforehand, etiquette requires that you pay whatever the driver asks on arrival. Even if the amount demanded is outrageous, he is right and it is your fault for not agreeing on a price beforehand. Bargaining has to take place *before* you accept a service or consume a product, not after.

6.03

Souvenirs

Handicrafts *Kerajinan*

keris ceremonial dagger	*dompét* wallet
kulit leather	*lukisan* painting
payung umbrella	*tas* bag/purse
wayang kulit flat shadow puppets (from animal hide)	

Woodcarvings *Ukiran kayu*

kayu wood

patung statue, sculpture

ukiran carving

topéng mask

wayang golék (Sundanese) wooden puppets

Textiles *Tékstil, Kain*

batik cap hand-printed batik
batik tulis hand-drawn batik
jumputan tie-dyed cloth
kain ikat ikat weavings   *kain* cloth
taplak méja table cloth   *sarung* sarong
seléndang shoulder-cloth for carrying babies, goods

6.04

Jewelry *Perhiasan*

emas gold   *pérak* silver
intan diamonds   *giok* jade
batu permata gems   *gelang* bracelet, bangle
anting earrings   *cincin* ring
kalung, rantai necklace, chain

T: *Mau tanya.*
   I would like to inquire.
   Kain ini dari mana?
   Where is this cloth from?

S: *Ini dari Sumatera.*
   This is from Sumatra.

T: *Sumatera di mana.*
   Where in Sumatra?

S: *Kain ini dari daérah Batak.*
   This cloth is from the Batak region.

T: *Patung ini baru atau lama?*
   Is this statue old or new?

S: *Kira-kira lima puluh tahun.*
   About 50 years (old).

6.05

Clothing *Pakaian, Baju*

baju, keméja shirt
celana dalam underpants
jaket jacket, windbreaker
jas sport jacket
kaus T-shirt
kaus kaki socks

blus blouse
celana pants
dasi tie
kaca, cermin mirror
kantong, saku pocket
kaus tangan gloves

pakaian clothing
pakaian dalam underwear
baju renang swimsuit

pas just right, fit, be the proper size
rok dress
sapu tangan handkerchief
sepatu shoes
sandal sandals, thongs (flipflops)
ukuran measurement, size

sabuk belt
seléndang scarf
setélan suit

topi hat

S: *Mau coba sepatu ini?* Would you like to try these shoes?

T: *Ya, saya mau coba yang hitam.*
Yes, I want to try the black ones.

S: *Ukuran berapa?* What is your size?

T: *Ukuran saya tiga puluh sembilan.*
My size is 39 (European sizes are the norm in Indonesia).

S: *Ini, coba dulu.* Here they are, please try them on.

T: *Sepatu ini terlalu kecil.* These shoes are too small.
Ada ukuran yang lebih besar? Do you have a larger size?

S: *Ada, sebentar.* Yes we do. Just a moment.

T: *Ya, ini sudah pas.* Yes, these fit just right.

Sundries

Photography *Fotografi*

afdruk, cétak print, photo print
kaméra, tustél camera
film film
film berwarna color film
memperbaiki to repair
cuci, mencuci to wash, develop (of film)

lénsa lens
rusak broken
betul correct, fixed

Stationery *Alat-alat tulis*

kertas paper
kertas tulis writing paper
tulis write
perangko stamps

amplop envelope
kartu pos postcard
pen, bolpoin pen
bloknot notepaper, writing pad

Reading material *Bahan bacaan*

6.07

buku book

toko buku bookstore

buku petunjuk (wisata) tourist guidebook

kamus dictionary

koran, surat kabar newspaper

koran berbahasa?

Inggris English newspaper

majalah magazine

peta map

roman, novél novel

Toiletries

6.08

tisu gulung toilet paper

sikat gigi toothbrush

sampo shampoo

pasta gigi, odol toothpaste

pembalut wanita sanitary pad

sabun soap

sisir comb

tampon tampon

tisu tissues

T: *Saya mau cétak foto.* I would like to print some photos.

S: *Mau dicétak berapa besar?*
What size would you like the prints?

T: *Yang biasa saja, 4R* (pronounced "*ér*". This is the standard A6 size). I would like the usual size, A6.

S: *Seperti ini.* Like this? (pointing)

T: *Ya, betul.* Correct.
Kapan selesai? When will they be ready?

S: *Satu jam lagi.* In one hour.

PART SEVEN

Things You Should Know

Telephone *Télepon*

7.01

Telephone service has improved greatly in Indonesia during the past decade, but it is still erratic. Exchanges are overloaded during peak hours. Numbers frequently change. Be patient and keep trying; eventually you will get through. Directory assistance is 108, for each local dialing code, eg. (021) 108 is directory assistance in Jakarta, (022) 108 is directory assistance in Bandung, etc.

> *télepon* telephone
> *nomor télepon* telephone number
> *menélepon* to telephone
> *hubungi, menghubungi* to contact, call

sambung connect

saluran connection

tekan, pencat press , dial (a phone)

kode (pronounced "KO-duh") code

kode negara country code

kode wilayah area code

pesawat extension number

interlokal, SLJJ (sambungan langsung jarak jauh)
long-distance (within Indonesia)

luar negeri, SLI (sambungan langsung internasional) overseas

dalam negeri domestic

 Note: Indonesians use the English word **Hello!** (spelled and pronounced *Halo!*) when answering the phone. When you ask to speak to someone, the person answering will normally ask who is calling by saying *Dari mana, ya?* (lit. "From where?") or *Dari siapa?* ("From who?"). You may either give your name or the place you are calling from.

Halo! Saya ingin télepon ke luar negeri, ke Amérika Serikat.
Hello! I would like to call overseas to the United States.

Tolong hubungi nomor ini. Please call this number.

Kode wilayah lima satu nol. Area code 510.

Nomornya empat nol lima tiga nol lima lima.
The number is 405-3055.

Tunggu sebentar. Please wait a moment.

Sedang bicara. The line is busy.

Coba sebentar lagi, ya. Try again in a moment, okay.

Silakan bicara. Please go ahead and speak.

Wah, tidak diangkat! Oh dear, there is no one there!

Putus. The line was cut off.

Boléh saya bicara dengan Ibu Suléiman, pesawat empat kosong dua? May I speak to Mrs. Suleiman, extension 402?

Dari mana, ya? Who is calling?

Dari Andrew. Andrew.

Halo, Bapak Subagio ada di rumah?
Hello, is Mr. Subagio at home?

Sedang keluar. He is out.

Kira-kira kapan kembali, ya?
Approximately when will he come back?

Coba télepon lagi jam dua siang.
Please call again at two o'clock this afternoon.

Halo. Ibu Siti ada? Hello. Is Siti there?

Ma'af, salah sambung! Sorry, wrong number!

Bapak tahu nomor yang baru tidak?
Do you know the new number or not?

Wah, saya tidak tahu. Oh my, I don't know.

Halo. Cari siapa, pak?
Hello. Whom do you wish to speak to, sir?

Saya cari Pak Affandi. I am looking for Pak Affandi.

Dari mana, ya? Who's calling, please?

Dari teman. A friend. (lit. "From a friend." Although you may hear this, this is not a recommended reply; it is better to state your name.)

Ada. Sebentar, saya panggil.
He is in. Just a moment, I will call him.

7.02

Post Office *Kantor Pos*

Post offices tend to be rather chaotic in Indonesia, and you will need to be a bit assertive to get things done quickly. First of all, find out which counters offer the services you want. Then fight your way through the crowd. Most counters sell stamps, but only certain ones will accept parcels, sell money orders, handle Poste Restante, etc. The following are a few helpful tips:

> Once you have bought stamps and stuck them onto a letter or package, return the item to the counter and watch as the stamps are cancelled.

> Mail is generally more secure and is delivered more promptly from a post office in a big city, so it is advisable to wait if you are in the countryside, if you can.

> Regular airmail usually takes about two weeks to North America or Europe; express airmail gets there a few days earlier.

pos post	*giro* postal money order
lokét counter	*biaya* cost
pakét parcel	*perangko* stamp
surat letter	

melalui by means of, via
pakai using, with, by

pos biasa normal (surface) mail

pos tercatat registered mail (this now includes express delivery)

pos udara airmail (overseas)

EMS (Express Mail Service) the fastest overseas service, but very expensive (supposed to take 2–3 days, but usually takes 4–5 days)

Mau tanya... I would like to inquire.

Di mana saya bisa beli perangko? Where can I buy stamps?

Di lokét dua atau tiga. At counters 2 or 3.

Di mana bisa kirim pakét ke luar negeri?
Where can I send a parcel overseas?

Di mana bisa kirim pakét ke luar negeri?
Where can I send a parcel overseas?

Di lokét tujuh. At counter 7.

Baiklah! Terima kasih.
Very well! Thank you.

Maaf, antri ya!
Get in line! (i.e. please don't cut in front of me!)

Saya mau kirim surat ini ke Australia melalui pos udara.
I would like to send this letter to Australia by airmail.

Biayanya berapa? What is the cost?

Sepuluh ribu rupiah. Rp. 10.000.

Kalau pakai EMS berapa? How much is it to use EMS?

Seratus ribu. Sampainya dalam waktu tiga hari.
Rp. 100.000, and it will take three days.

Baiklah! Saya pakai pos udara saja.
Very well! I'll use airmail.

Ada dua surat dan satu kartu pos.
I have two letters and one postcard.

Bank

7.03

bank bank	***cabang*** branch
uang money	***uang kecil*** small change
uang récéh, uang logam coins	
uang kertas banknotes	
uang tunai cash	***kurs*** exchange rate
transfer to transfer	***tukar, menukar*** to exchange

Saya mau tukar uang dolar Amérika.
I would like to change American dollars.

Kursnya berapa hari ini? What is the exchange rate today?

Kursnya delapan ribu lima ratus rupiah. The rate is Rp. 8.500.

Saya mau tukar seratus dolar. I want to change $100.

7.04

Customs and Police

bagasi baggage, luggage	*pabéan, béa cukai* customs
koper suitcase	*lapor* declare, report
tas bag	*polisi* police
dompét purse, wallet	*kantor polisi* police station
curi, mencuri to steal	*formulir* forms
copét pickpocket	*maling* thief

At customs:

Bag asi ini punya siapa? Whose luggage is this?

Punya saya. It is mine.

Ada apa di dalam? What is inside?

Pakaian saja. Just clothing.

Tidak ada barang untuk dilaporkan.
I have nothing to declare.

At the police station:

Pak, saya kehilangan tas/dompét.
Sir, I have lost my purse/wallet.

Di mana? Where?

Baru tadi, di setasiun keréta api.
Just now, at the train station.

Apakah melihat siapa yang ambil?
Did you see who took it?

Tidak. Barangkali copét. No. Probably a pickpocket.

Baik! Ini ada formulir. Very well! Here is a form.

Harus diisi dulu. You must fill it out first.

Having to deal with the government bureaucracy in Indonesia can be a rather trying experience. The only recommendations we can make are patience, persistence, asking as many questions as possible, and more patience.

If you seem to be having trouble getting something done, ask *Siapa yang bertanggung jawab dalam?* "Who has responsibility in this matter?" and don't be satisfied until you find the person in charge.

It never does any good to get angry, however. Keep your cool and explain your position firmly and clearly, repeating it several times. Make sure you understand the procedures being applied, and don't expect anything to happen very quickly! The preparation and signing of documents alone can take several days.

Filling Out Forms *Mengisi formulir*

7.05

The following are common entries on immigration and other forms, such as in hotels. These are often in English.

nama name	*alamat* residence
tanggal date	*umur* age
kelamin sex	*agama* religion
pekerjaan occupation	
tempat lahir place of birth	
kebangsaan nationality	
maksud kunjungan purpose of visit	
status (kawin) marital status	
tanda tangan signature	

7.06

Health and Illness

Sakit is the all-purpose term for "sickness" or "pain", while *obat* is similarly used to denote any type of medicine or treatment. If you are sick, it is easy and inexpensive to consult a doctor and obtain a prescription in Indonesia. Consultation hours are during the afternoons and evenings, from 4 pm onwards. At other times, and in case of emergency, you are better off going to the emergency ward (UGD or IGD) of a hospital. Many doctors speak a bit of English. The normal procedure for flu or stomach ailments, however, is to issue antibiotics without running any tests to see what is causing the problem. If you have serious stomach problems, it is better to go directly to a laboratory and give them stool and urine samples. They will then refer you to a doctor if the tests are positive. Pharmacies are usually very well stocked, but most brand names are different in Indonesia, so ask your doctor to note down the generic names of any prescription drugs you may require before you leave. Some prescription drugs are sold over the counter in Indonesia.

sakit sick	*séhat* healthy
sakit gigi toothache	*sakit kepala* headache
sakit peru stomach ache	*sakit maag* indigestion
sakit tenggorokan sore throat	
parah serious (of illness)	
dokter doctor	*dokter gigi* dentist
dokter anak pediatrician, children's doctor	
dokter héwan veterinarian	
dokter mata opthalmologist	
dokter THT ear, nose and throat specialist	
rumah sakit hospital	*kecelakaan* accident
ambulans ambulance	*darurat* emergency
unit gawat darurat emergency room (in a hospital)	
laboratorium laboratory	
juru rawat, perawat, suster nurse	

batuk cough   *demam* fever

diaré, bérak-bérak, méncért diarrhoea

hamil pregnant   *lécét* cut; blister

luka injury, injured   *muntah* vomit

patah tulang broken bone, break a bone

pilek, masuk angin, flu cold, flu

keracunan makanan food poisoning

pusing dizziness, nausea   *racun* poison

obat medicine

apotik pharmacy, drugstore   *antibiotik* antibiotics

aspirin aspirin   *pléster* bandage, band-aid

resép prescription   *suntik, injéksi* injection

Saya sakit. Ada dokter di sini yang bisa bahasa Inggeris?
I am sick. Is there a doctor here (i.e. nearby) who speaks English?

Saya mau ke rumah sakit. I want to go to hospital.

Tolong panggil ambulans. Please call an ambulance.

Saya mau beli obat.
I want to buy some medicine.

Di mana ada apotik?
Where is a pharmacy?

Ini resépnya.
Here is the prescription.

Ada obat untuk batuk?
Do you have cough medicine?

Ada obat untuk pilek?
Do you have cold medicine?

Ada obat untuk sakit perut?
Do you have medicine for stomach ailments?

7.07

Parts of the Body

darah blood	*otot* muscle
urat tendon	

kepala head	*mata* eye, eyes
pipi cheeks	*rahang* jaw
mulut mouth	*lidah* tongue
gigi tooth, teeth	*hidung* nose
rambut hair	*léhér* neck
telinga ear, ears	*ténggorokan* throat

badan body	*bahu, pundak* shoulder, shoulders
dada chest	*payudara* breasts
pinggang waist	*perut* stomach, belly
punggung back	

lengan arm	*tangan* hand, arm
jari tangan fingers	*kuku* nails
kaki leg, foot	*jari kaki* toe, toes

pergelangan kaki, mata kaki ankle
pergelangan tangan wrist

kemaluan genitals	*rahim* womb, uterus
kulit skin	*tulang* bone

Verb and Noun Affixes

Indonesian has many words that are derived from simple roots through the addition of prefixes and suffixes. For example, the word *baik* alone means "good" and serves as the root for *kebaikan* (with prefix *ke-* and suffix *-an*) meaning "goodness." *Memperbaiki* (using the *memper-* prefix and *-i* object suffix) means "to improve (something)", while the noun *perbaikan* (*per-* and *-an*) means "improvement" or "correction." When dealing with derived forms, you need to know the mechanical rules for adding prefixes and suffixes to root words. Then you are able to identify roots of words you come across so you can look them up in a dictionary. Second, you need to understand how the addition of these various prefixes and suffixes changes the meaning of a root. Not every affix can be used for every root. As with any language, you need to learn the vocabulary, but understanding the affix system helps learners of Indonesian greatly. You will find that it is quite logical, and that you will be able to guess the meanings of many new words.

Verb Affixes

The active prefix *meN–* (for transitive verbs)

Most transitive verbs (verbs which can take a direct object) may be prefixed by *meN-* (where *N* stands for various letters, depending on the first letter of the root word that follows). This prefix generally does not change the meaning of the root, but merely emphasizes that a verb is being used in an active (as opposed to passive) sense, i.e. that the subject of the verb is the main focus or topic of the sentence.

>*lihat* ⇒ *melihat* to see

>*Saya sudah melihat Borobudur.* I have already seen Borobudur.

In some cases, the addition of *meN-* dramatically alters the meaning of the root word, as in the example of *tinggal* ("stay; leave") ⇒ *meninggal* ("die, pass away"), where the latter is a shortened form of *meninggal dunia* meaning "to depart the world."

As already mentioned in Part Two: A Quick Word About Grammar, in colloquial speech the prefix is usually omitted. Note also that this prefix is rarely used in imperatives.

This active verb prefix is also used to create verbs out of nouns and adjectives. In this case the root and the prefixed form have quite different, although related, meanings.

>*kuning* yellow ⇒ *menguning* to turn yellow

>*kipas* a fan ⇒ *mengipasi* to fan

>*kunci* a key ⇒ *mengunci* to lock

meN– forms

The prefix *meN-* takes five different forms, depending on the first letter of the word that it is prefixed to. You will need to memorize the following rules for this.

>1) *meny-* for words beginning with *s-*
>
>>*siram* ⇒ *menyiram* to spray, shower
>>
>>*surat* a letter ⇒ *menyurat* to write a letter

>2) *mem-* before words beginning with *b-* and *p-*
>
>>*beli* ⇒ *membeli* to buy
>>
>>*pakai* ⇒ *memakai* to use
>>
>>NB. This last form changes the initial *-p* of the base word to a *-m.*

3) **men-** for words beginning with **d-, j-, c-** and **t**

    dorong ⇒ *mendorong* to push

    jual ⇒ *menjual* to sell

    cuci ⇒ *mencuci* to wash

    tonton ⇒ *menonton* to watch (a movie, show)

    NB. This last form changes the initial *-t* of the base word to a *-n*.

4) **meng-** for words beginning with **k, g, h** or any vowel

    kirim ⇒ *mengirim* to send

    NB. This last form removes the initial *-k* of the base word.

    ganggu ⇒ *mengganggu* to disturb

    harap ⇒ *mengharapkan* to hope

    atur ⇒ *mengatur* to arrange

5) **me-** before all other initial consonants

    lukis ⇒ *melukis* to paint

    mula ⇒ *memulai* to begin

    nikah ⇒ *menikah* to marry

    rusak ⇒ *merusak* to damage

    warna ⇒ *mewarnai* to color (in)

The active prefix *ber–* (for intransitive verbs)

The active prefix *ber-* is used with intransitive verbs (those which cannot take a direct object) in much the same way that *me-* is prefixed to transitive verbs. As with the *meN-* prefix, it is often omitted in everyday speech.

    asal ⇒ *berasal* to originate

    bicara ⇒ *berbicara* to speak

    diri ⇒ *berdiri* to stand

kunjung ⇒ *berkunjung* to pay a visit

Saya ingin berkunjung ke rumah anda.
I wish to pay a visit to your house.

Kami berasal dari Australia. We are from Australia.

 Note: That there are a number of irregular forms.

ajar teach ⇒ *belajar* to learn

kerja ⇒ *bekerja* to work

When prefixed to a noun, *ber-* creates an active, intransitive verb that has the meaning "possessing" or "taking the attribute of" that noun or adjective.

kembang blossom, flower ⇒ *berkembang* to develop, blossom, expand

bahasa language ⇒ *berbahasa* to know or speak a language

pakaian clothing ⇒ *berpakaian* to get dressed, be dressed

kata words ⇒ *berkata* to speak

Koran ini tidak berbahasa Indonesia.
This newspaper is not in Indonesian.

 Note: Before words beginning with *r, ber-* becomes *be-* (which is to say that only one *r* appears in the resulting prefixed form).

renang ⇒ *berenang* to swim

rencana ⇒ *berencana* to plan

The passive prefix *di–*

The opposite of the active prefix *meN-* is the passive prefix *di-* which indicates that the object of the verb is the main focus or topic of the sentence. This is very similar to the passive voice in English. (See Part Two: Grammar for more examples with *di-*.)

> *Mobilnya belum diperbaiki.* The car has not yet *been repaired.*
>
> *Kita diundang ke pésta.* We *have been invited* to a party.
>
> *Nasinya sudah dimasak.* The rice *has* already *been cooked.*

The perfective prefix *ter–*

The prefix *ter-* is used to indicate that an action has already been completed, with the emphasis being on the resultant state or condition of the direct object. As with *di-* the focus or main topic of the sentence is always the object of the verb and not the subject. In fact the subject is often not even mentioned when *ter-* is used, as it is either understood, unimportant or intentionally left ambiguous.

> *kenal* know, be acquainted ⇒ *terkenal* to be famous, well-known
>
> *atur* arrange ⇒ *teratur* to be well-organized, neat
>
> *pakai* use ⇒ *terpakai* to have been used

This prefix is often used together with the word *sudah* meaning "already."

> *Kamarnya sudah terkunci.* The room is already locked.
>
> *Bon kami sudah terbayar belum?* Has our bill been paid yet?

 Note: The use of *ter-* as a verb prefix is distinct from the use of *ter-* with adjectives, in which case it forms a superlative meaning the most, the greatest, etc. (See Part Two: Grammar.)

The affix *meN–kan*

The verb affix *meN-kan* creates transitive verbs out of intransitive verbs as well as nouns and adjectives.

> *selesai* finished ⇒ *menyelesaikan* to finish or settle something
>
> *tinggal* stay, leave ⇒ *meninggalkan* to leave something behind
>
> *kata* words ⇒ *mengatakan* to speak, say
>
> *pasar* market ⇒ *memasarkan* to market (goods, etc.)
>
> *betul* correct ⇒ *membetulkan* to correct

When **-kan** is added to a verb that is already transitive, it may indicate that the action is being focused on the direct object of the verb. **-kan** can also be used in the sense of a request.

> *Tolong bukakan pintu.* Please open the door (for me).

Suffixed forms with **-kan** may be used in an active sense with **me-** (although the latter is often dropped in everyday speech), or in a passive sense with **di-**.

> *Saya belum menyelesaikan pekerjaan itu.*
> I haven't finished that work yet.
>
> *Kaméra ini bisa diperbaiki tidak?*
> Can this camera be fixed or not?

The dative suffix *–i*

The dative suffix *-i* is added to intransitive verbs and adjectives to create transitive verbs which imply that something is being done to, toward, for the benefit of, or by the subject. It often conveys a strong sense of location or direction.

> *awas* careful, alert ⇒ *awasi* to guard, watch over
>
> *datang* come ⇒ *datangi* to pay a visit to someone
>
> *pinjam* borrow ⇒ *pinjami* to lend
>
> *dekat* close, nearby ⇒ *dekati* to approach
>
> *hubung* connect ⇒ *hubungi* to contact, get in touch with

Resulting verbs with *-i* can be used both in an active sense with *me-*, and in a passive sense with *di-*.

Soya akan coba menghubungi anda di kantor.
I will try to contact you at the office.

Tolong barang saya dijaga sebentar.
Please look after my things for a moment.

The causative prefix *memper–*

The prefix *memper-* is a causative prefix added to adjectives to form transitive verbs.

> *kecil* small ⇒ *memperkecil* to reduce, make smaller
>
> *besar* large ⇒ *memperbesar* to enlarge
>
> *panjang* long ⇒ *memperpanjang* to extend

It is most often used together with the suffixes *-i* and *-kan* to produce transitive verbs that indicate that the subject of the sentence is instrumental in bringing about the action or state intended. The form *memper-* is used in the active sense, while *diper-* is used in the passive sense. The suffix *-i* is most often used with adjectives and in transitive verb roots, while *-kan* is used with transitive verb roots (but also with some adjectives). The usages of *-i* and *-kan* in these constructions are quite irregular and actually vary with different dialects of Indonesian.

lihat see ⇒ *memperlihatkan* to show (something to someone)

ingat remember ⇒ *memperingati* to commemorate

kenal know, be acquainted ⇒ *memperkenalkan* to introduce (to someone)

timbang weigh ⇒ *mempertimbangkan* to consider

baik good, well ⇒ *memperbaiki* to improve, fix, repair

Noun Affixes

There are a number of different ways of producing nouns out of verbs and adjectives, and even from other nouns.

The instrumental prefix *pe*–

The instrumental prefix *pe-* is added to nouns or verbs to produce nouns meaning "one who does" something.

laut sea ⇒ *pelaut* sailor

main play ⇒ *pemain* player

Rules for prefixing *peN–*

As with *meN-*, the prefix *peN-* takes five different forms depending on the initial letter of the verb or noun it is attached to. These correspond with the individual *meN-* form for each initial letter.

1) *peny-* before words beginning with *s*

   sakit sick, ill ⇒ *penyakit* illness

2) *pem-* before words beginning with *b-* and *p*

   beli buy ⇒ *pembeli* buyer

   pakai use ⇒ *pemakai* user

3) *pen-* for words beginning with *d-*, *j-*, *c-* and *t*

   dengar hear ⇒ *pendengar* listener

   curi steal ⇒ *pencuri* thief

   tonton watch ⇒ *penonton* viewer

4) *peng-* for words beginning with *k*, *g* or any vowel

   karang to write ⇒ *pengarang* author

   ganti to exchange ⇒ *pengganti* replacement

   urus to arrange ⇒ *pengurus* person in charge

5) *pe-* before all other initial consonants

Note: In the examples given above, as with *meN-*, the first letters *p*, *t*, *k* and *s* of the root verbs are dropped when the prefix is added.

The suffix –an

The suffix *-an* is added to verbs to produce nouns.

> *makan* eat ⇒ *makanan* food
>
> *minum* drink ⇒ *minuman* a drink
>
> *pinjam* borrow ⇒ *pinjaman* borrowings
>
> *tegur* warn ⇒ *teguran* warning
>
> *kenal* know, be acquainted ⇒ *kenalan* acquaintance

The circumfix *peN–* + *–an*

The nominalizing circumfix *pe-* + *-an* also changes verbs to nouns. It generally indicates a process taking place.

> *periksa* inspect ⇒ *pemeriksaan* inspection, act of inspecting
>
> *terima* receive ⇒ *penerimaan* receipts
>
> *bicara* talk ⇒ *pembicaraan* discussions
>
> *harap* hope ⇒ *harapan, pengharapan* hope, expectation
>
> *labuh* drop anchor ⇒ *pelabuhan* harbor, port

Rules for adding *peN-* here are the same as those given above.

The circumfix *per–* + *–an*

The circumfix *per-* + *-an* indicates nouns, often abstract.

> *coba* try ⇒ *percobaan* test, attempt
>
> *kawin* marry ⇒ *perkawinan* wedding
>
> *kembang* flower, blossom ⇒ *perkembangan* development

The circumfix *ke–* + *–an*

The circumfix *ke-* + *-an* is added to verbs and adjectives to produce abstract nouns.

ada be, exist ⇒ *keadaan* state, condition

aman secure, safe ⇒ *keamanan* security

nyata clear, evident ⇒ *kenyataan* facts, evidence

baik good, well ⇒ *kebaikan* goodness

besar large ⇒ *kebesaran* size, largeness

APPENDIX B

Suggestions for Further Study

To improve your vocabulary and language in general, watch television and buy a couple of Indonesian magazines. Flashcards are quite useful and can be carried everywhere.

We recommend the Tuttle series of Indonesian-English dictionaries: *Tuttle Concise Indonesian Dictionary* by A.L. Kramer, revised by Katherine Davidsen, and *Tuttle Pocket Indonesian Dictionary* and *Tuttle Compact Indonesian Dictionary*, both compiled by Katherine Davidsen.

Bilingual Dictionaries

English-Indonesian Dictionary

For the sake of clarity, only the most common Indonesian equivalents for each English word have been given below.

In the case of verbs, simple roots are given first, followed by common affixed form(s) with the same meaning, if any. For more on affixation of verbal roots, see Appendix A.

A

able to *bisa*

about (approximately) *kira-kira, sekitar*

about (regarding) *tentang, mengenai*

above, upstairs *di atas*

accident *kecelakaan*

accidentally, by chance *kebetulan*

accommodation *penginapan*

accompany, to *ikut, mendampingi*

according to *menurut*

acquainted, to be *kenai, mengenal*

across from *seberang*

act, to *tindak, bertindak*

action *tindakan*

active *giat*

activity *kegiatan*

add to *tambah, menambah*

address *alamat*

admit, confess *akui, mengakui*

advance money, deposit *uang muka*

advance, go forward *maju*

afraid *takut, ngeri*

after *sesudah, setelah*

afternoon (3 pm to dusk) *soré*

afternoon (midday) *siang*

afterwards, then *kemudian*

again *lagi*

age *umur*

agree to do something, to *janji, berjanji*

agree, to *setujui, menyetujui*

agreed! *setuju! jadi!*

agreement *perjanjian, persetujuan*

air *udara*

airplane *pesawat, kapal terbang*

alive *hidup*

all *semua, seluruh, segala*

alley, lane *gang*

allow, permit *biarkan, perboléhkan*

allowed to (= may) *boléh*

almost *hampir*

alone *sendiri, sendirian*

already *sudah*

also *juga*

ambassador *duta besar*

among *antara, di antara*

amount *jumlah, sejumlah*

ancient *kuno*

and *dan*

angle *segi*

angry *marah*

animal *binatang*

annoyed *kesal*

answer the phone *angkat télepon*

answer, response (spoken) *jawaban*

answer, respond, to (a letter) *balas, membalas*

answer, to respond (spoken) *jawab, menjawab*

ape *kera, monyet*

appear, to *muncul, memuncul; timbul*

appearance, looks *rupa, penampilan*

apple *apel*

approach, to (in space) *mendekati*

approach, to (in time) *menjelang*

approximately *kira-kira, sekitar*

April *bulan April*

area *wilayah, daerah*

arena *gelanggang*

arm, hand *lengan*

army *tentara*

around (approximately) *kira-kira, sekitar*

around (nearby) *dekat*

around (surrounding) *sekeliling, di sekitar*

arrange, to *atur, mengatur: urus, mengurus*

arrangements, planning *perencanaan*

arrival *ketibaan, kedatangan*

arrive, to *tiba, datang*

art *seni*

artist *seniman*

ashamed, embarrassed *malu*

ask about, to *tanyakan, menanyakan*

ask for, request *minta, meminta*

ask, to *tanya, bertanya*

assemble, gather *kumpul, berkumpul*

assemble, put together, to *pasang, memasang*

assist, to *bantu, membantu*

assistance *bantuan*

astonished *kaget, heran*

at *di* (place), *pada* (time)

atmosphere, ambience *suasana*

attain, reach *capai, mencapai, sampai*

attend, to *hadir*

attitude *sikap*
auction, to *lelang, melelang*
auctioned off *dilelang*
August *bulan Agustus*
aunt *bibi, tante*
authority, person in charge
  orang yang berwajib
authority, power *kekuasaan*
automobile *mobil*
available *sedia, tersedia*
available, to make *sediakan,*
  menyediakan
average (numbers) *rata-rata*
average (so-so, just okay)
  lumayan, sedang
awake, to *bangun*
awaken, to *membangunkan*
aware *sadar*
awareness *kesadaran*

B

baby *bayi*
back *belakang*
back of *di belakang*
back up, to *mundur, ngatret*
backwards, reversed *terbalik*
bad *jelek*
bad luck *celaka, malang*
bag *tas*
baggage *bagasi, kopor*
ball *bola*
banana *pisang*
bargain, to *tawar, menawar*
base, foundation *dasar*
based on *berdasar*

basic *dasar, umum*
basis *dasar*
basket *keranjang*
bath *mandi*
bathe, to take a bath *mandi*
bathroom *kamar mandi*, WC
  ("way-say")
bay *teluk*
be, exist, have *ada*
beach *pantai*
bean *kacang*
beat (to defeat) *kalahkan,*
  mengalahkan
beat (to strike) *pukul*
beautiful (of people) *cakap,*
  cantik
beautiful (of places) *indah*
beautiful (of things) *bagus*
because *karena, sebab*
become, to *jadi, menjadi*
bed *tempat tidur*
bedroom *kamar tidur*
bedsheet *seprei*
beef *daging sapi*
before (in front of) *di depan, di*
  muka
before (in time) *sebelum*
beforehand, earlier *dulu*
begin, to *mulai, memulai*
beginning *permulaan*
beginning, in the *awalnya*
behind *di belakang*
belief, faith *kepercayaan*
believe, to *percaya, yakin*
below, downstairs *di bawah*
belt *sabuk*

best *paling baik, paling bagus*

better *lebih baik, lebih bagus*

between *antara*

bicycle *sepéda*

big (area) *luas*

big (size) *besar*

bill *bon, rékening*

billion *milyar*

bird *burung*

birth, to give *melahirkan*

birthday *hari ulang tahun*

bitter *pahit*

black *hitam*

blanket *selimut*

blood *darah*

blossom *kembang*

blouse *blus*

blue *biru*

boat *perahu*

body *badan, tubuh*

boil, to *merebus*

boiled *rebus*

bone *tulang*

book *buku*

border, edge *perbatasan, pinggir*

bored *bosan*

boring *membosankan*

born *lahir*

borrow, to *pinjam, meminjam*

botanic gardens *kebun raya, taman raya*

both *dua-duanya, keduanya*

bother, disturb *ganggu, mengganggu*

bother, disturbance *gangguan*

boundary, border *perbatasan*

bowl *mangkok*

box (cardboard) *kardos, dos*

box *kotak*

boy *anak laki-laki*

boyfriend *pucar*

bracelet *gelang*

branch *cabang*

brand *cap, merek*

brave, daring *berani*

bread *roti*

break apart, to *bongkar, membongkar*

break down, to (of cars, machines) *mogok*

break off, to *putus*

break up, divorce *cerai*

break, shatter *pecah, memecahkan*

bridge *jembatan*

bring, to *bawa, membawa*

broad, spacious *luas*

broadcast, program *siaran*

broadcast, to *siarkan, menyiarkan*

broken off *putus*

broken, does not work, spoiled *rusak*

broken, shattered *pecah*

broken, snapped (of bones, etc.) *patah*

broom *sapu*

broth, soup *kuah*

brother *saudara*

brother, older *kakak (laki-laki)*

brother, younger *adik*

brother-in-law *ipar*
brown *coklat*
brush *sikat*
brush, to *sikat, menyikat, gosok, menggosok*
buffalo (water buffalo) *kerbau*
build, to *bangun, membangun*
building *gedung*
burn, burnt *bakar*
burned down, out *terbakar*
bus *bis*
bus station *terminal bis*
business *bisnis, perdagangan*
businessman *pedagang*
busy, crowded *ramai*
busy, to be *sibuk*
but *tetapi*
butter *mentéga*
butterfly *kupu-kupu*
buy *beli, membeli*
by *oléh*

C

cabbage *kol*
cabbage, Chinese *cai sim*
cake, pastry *kue*
call on the telephone *télepon, menélepon*
call, summon *panggil, memanggil*
calm *tenang*
can, be able to *bisa*
can, tin *kaleng*
cancel *membatalkan*
candle *lilin*

candy *permén*
capable of, to be *sanggup*
capture, to *tangkap, menangkap*
car, automobile *mobil*
card *kartu*
care for, love *sayang, menyayangi*
care of, to take *mengasuh, mengawasi, menjaga*
careful! *hati-hati! awas!*
carrot *wortel*
carry, to *bawa, membawa*
cart (horsecart) *dokar, kereta kuda*
cart (pushcart) *gerobak, kereta*
carve, to *ukir, mengukir*
carving *ukiran*
cash money *uang tunai, uang kontan*
cash a check, to *menguangkan*
cast, throw out *buang, membuang*
cat *kucing*
catch, to *tangkap, menangkap*
cauliflower *kembang kol*
cave *gua*
celebrate, to *merayakan*
celery *seledri*
center *pusat, tengah*
central *pusat*
ceremony *upacara*
certain *pasti, tentu*
certainly! *memang!*
chain *rantai*
chair *kursi*
challenge *tantangan*
champion *juara*

chance, to have an opportunity to *sempat*

chance, by accident *kebetulan*

chance, opportunity *kesempatan*

change, small *uang kecil*

change, to (of conditions, situations) *berubah*

change, exchange (money, opinions) *tukar, menukar*

change, switch (clothes, things) *ganti, mengganti*

character *watak*

characteristic *sifat*

chase away, chase out *usir, mengusir*

chase, to *kejar, mengejar*

cheap *murah*

cheat, someone who cheats *penipu*

cheat, to *tipu, menipu*

cheek *pipi*

cheese *kéju*

chess *catur*

chest (box) *peti*

chest (breast) *dada*

chicken *ayam*

child *anak*

chili pepper *cabe, lombok*

chili sauce *sambal*

chocolate *cokelat*

choice *pilihan*

choose, to *pilih, memilih*

chopsticks *sumpit*

church *geréja*

cigarette *rokok*

cinema *bioskop*

citizen *warga negara*

citrus *jeruk*

city *kota*

clarification *penjelasan*

clarify, to *menjelaskan*

class, category *golongan, tipe, jenis*

classes (at university) *kuliah*, (at school) *mata pelajaran*

clean *bersih*

clean, to *bersihkan, membersihkan*

cleanliness *kebersihan*

clear *jelas, terang*

clear (of weather) *cerah, terang*

clever *cerdik, pintar*

climate *iklim*

climb onto, into *naik*

climb up (of hills, mountains) *mendaki*

clock *jam*

close together, tight *rapat*

close to, nearby *dekat*

close, to cover *menutup*

closed *tutup*

cloth *kain*

clothes, clothing *pakaian, baju*

cloudy, overcast *mendung*

clove *cengkeh*

clove cigarette *krétek*

coarse, to be *kasar*

coconut *kelapa*

coffee *kopi*

cold *pilek, masuk angin*

cold *dingin*

colleague *rekan*

collect payment, to *tagih*, *menagih*

color *warna*

comb *sisir*

come in, to *masuk*

come on, let's go *ayo, mari*

come, to *datang*

command, order *perintah*

command, to *perintah*, *memerintah*

company *perusahaan*

compare, to *membandingkan*

compared to *dibandingkan*

compete, to *bersaing; menyaingi*

competition *saingan*

complain, to *mengeluh*

complaint *keluhan*

complete, finish something *selesaikan, menyelesaikan*

complete, to be *lengkap*

complete, to make *selesaikan, menyelesaikan*

completed, finished *selesai*

complicated *rumit*

compose, write (letters, books, music) *karang, mengarang*

composition, writing *karangan*

concerning *tentang, mengenai*

condition (pre-condition) *syarat*

condition (status) *keadaan*

confidence *kepercayaan*

confidence, to have *percaya*

confuse, to *membuat bingung, membingungkan*

confused (in a mess) *kacau*

confused (mentally) *bingung*

confusing *membingungkan*

congratulations! *selamat!*

connect together, to *sambung, menyambung*

connection *hubungan, sambungan*

conscious of, to be *sadari, menyadari*

consider (to have an opinion) *anggap, menganggap*

consider (to think over) *pertimbangkan, mempertimbangkan*

consult, talk over with *rundingkan, merundingkan*

contact, connection *hubungan*

contact, get in touch with *hubungi, menghubungi*

continue, to *teruskan, meneruskan*

cook, to *masak, memasak*

cooked, ripe *masak, matang*

cookie *kue*

cooking, cuisine *masakan*

cool *sejuk*

coral (rock) *batu karang*

corn *jagung*

cost (expense) *ongkos, biaya*

cost (price) *harga*

cotton *kapas*

cough *batuk*

count, reckon *hitung, menghitung*

counter, window (for paying money, buying tickets) *loket*

country *negara*

cover, to *tutup, menutup*

crab *kepiting*
cracked *retak*
cracker, biscuit *biskuit*
crafts *kerajinan*
craftsman *tukang*
crate *peti*
crazy *gila*
criminal *penjahat*
crowded *ramai*
cruel *kejam, bengis*
cry out, to *teriak, berteriak*
cry, to *tangis, menangis*
cucumber *timun, mentimun*
culture *kebudayaan*
cup *cangkir, gelas, tempat minum*
cured, well *sembuh*
custom, tradition *adat*
customer *langganan*
cut, slice *potongan*
cut, to *potong, memotong*

D

dance *tarian*
dance, to *tari, menari*
danger *bahaya*
dangerous *berbahaya*
daring, brave *berani*
dark *gelap*
date (of the month) *tanggal*
daughter *anak perempuan*
daughter-in-law *menantu*
day *hari*
day after tomorrow *lusa*
daybreak *fajar*

dazed, dizzy *pusing*
dead *mati*
debt *utang*
deceive, to *tipu, menipu*
December *bulan Desember*
decide, to *memutuskan*
decision *keputusan*
decrease, to *berkurang; kurangi, mengurangi*
deer *rusa*
defeat, to *kalahkan, mengalahkan*
defecate, to *buang air besar, bérak*
defect *cacat*
degree, level *nilai*
degrees (temperature) *derajat*
delicious *sedap, enak, lezat*
demand, to *tuntut, menuntut*
depart, to *berangkat, tinggal, pergi*
depend on *tergantung; bergantung pada*
deposit, leave behind with someone *titip, menitip*
deposit, put money in the bank *menyetor (uang)*
describe, to *gambarkan, menggambarkan*
desire *keinginan, nafsu*
desire, to *ingin, kepingin*
destination *tujuan*
destroy, to *hancurkan, menghancurkan*
destroyed, ruined *hancur*
determined, stubborn *keras kepala*

develop, to *berkembang; mengembangkan*

develop, to (film) *cuci cetak, mencuci cetak*

development *perkembangan; pembangunan*

diamond *intan, berlian*

dictionary *kamus*

die, to *mati, meninggal, wafat*

difference (discrepancy in figures) *selisih*

difference (in quality) *perbédaan, béda*

different, other *lain, béda*

difficult *sukar, sulit, susah*

dipper, ladle *gayung*

direct, non-stop *langsung*

direction *jurusan, arah*

dirt, filth *kotoran*

dirty *kotor*

disaster, disastrous *celaka*

discrepancy *selisih*

discuss, to *bicarakan, membicarakan*

discussion *pembicaraan*

display *pajangan*

display, to *pajangkan, memajangkan*

distance *jarak*

disturb, to *ganggu, mengganggu*

disturbance *gangguan*

divide, split up *bagi-bagi, membagi*

division *pembagian*

divorce, to *cerai, bercerai; menceraikan*

divorced *cerai*

dizzy, ill *pusing*

do not *jangan*

do one's best *berusaha*

do, perform an action *melakukan*

doctor *dokter*

document, letter *surat*

dog *anjing*

dolphin *lumba-lumba*

done (cooked) *masak, matang*

done (finished) *selesai*

door *pintu*

doubt something, to *ragu-ragu, meragukan*

doubtful *ragu-ragu*

down, to come or go down, get off *turun*

down, to take down *turunkan, menurunkan*

downtown *pusat kota, tengah kota*

draw, to *gambar, meng gambar*

drawer *laci*

drawing *gambar*

dream *impian, mimpi*

dream, to *mimpi, bermimpi*

dress, skirt *rok*

dressed, to get *berpakaian, ganti baju*

drink, refreshment *minuman*

drink, to *minum*

drive, to (a car) *menyupir, setir, menyetir*

driver *supir*

drowned *tenggelam*

drug, medicine *obat*

drugstore *apotik*

drunk *mabuk*
dry *kering*
dry (season) *kemarau*
dry out (in the sun) *jemur*
duck *bébék*
dusk *senja*
dust *debu*
duty (import tax) *béa cukai*
duty (responsibility) *kewajiban,
tugas*

E

each, every *setiap, tiap-tiap*
ear *kuping, telinga*
earlier, beforehand *dulu*
early *pagi, cepat, dini, lebih awal*
early in the morning *pagi-pagi*
Earth, the World *bumi*
earth, soil *tanah*
east *timur*
easy *gampang, mudah*
eat, to *makan*
echo *gema*
economical *hemat*
economy *ekonomi*
edge *pinggir, batas*
educate, to *didik, mendidik*
education *pendidikan*
effort *usaha*
effort, to make an *berusaha*
egg *telur*
eggplant *térong*
eight *delapan*
electric, electricity *listrik*
elephant *gajah*

eleven *sebelas*
embarrassed *malu*
embarrassing *memalukan*
embassy *kedutaan besar
(kedubes)*
emergency *darurat*
empty *kosong*
end, tip *ujung*
enemy *musuh*
energy *tenaga*
enlarge, to *perbesar, memperbesar*
enough *cukup*
enter, to *masuk*
entire *seluruh*
entirety, whole *keseluruhan*
envelope *sampul*
envy, envious *iri (hati)*
equal *seimbang, sama*
equality *keseimbangan,
persamaan*
especially *khusus*
establish, set up *mendirikan*
estimate, to *tafsir, menafsir*
ethnic group *(suku) bangsa*
even (also) *juga*
even (smooth) *rata, mulus*
ever, have already *pernah*
every kind of *segala macam*
every *tiap, segala*
every time *tiap kali*
exact, exactly *tepat*
exactly! just so! *persis!*
exam, test *ujian*
examine, to *periksa, memeriksa*
example *umpama, misal*

example, for *umpamanya, misalnya*

except *kecuali*

exchange rate *kurs*

exchange, to (money,opinions) *tukar, menukar*

excuse me! *permisi!*

exit *keluar*

expand, grow larger *berkembang*

expect, to *harapkan, mengharapkan*

expect, to *mengharap*

expense *biaya*

expensive *mahal, méwah*

expensive *mahal*

expert *ahli*

express, state *ucapkan, mengucapkan*

extend, to *perpanjang, memperpanjang*

extremely *sangat*

eye *mata*

eyeglasses *kacamata*

F

face *muka, wajah*

face, to *hadapi, menghadapi*

fail, to *gagal*

failure *kegagalan*

fall (season) *musim gugur*

fall, to *jatuh*

false (imitation) *tiruan*

false (not true) *keliru*

falsify, to *tiru, meniru*

family *keluarga*

fan (admirer) *penggemar*

fan (used for cooling) *kipas*

fancy *méwah*

far *jauh*

fart, to *kentut*

fast *cepat, lekas*

fat, grease *lemak*

fat, to be *gemuk*

father *bapak, ayah*

father-in-law *mertua*

fault, to *salahkan, menyalahkan; salahi, menyalahi*

fear *takut*

February *bulan Februari*

feel, to *rasa, berasa, merasa*

feeling *perasaan, rasa*

fertile *subur*

fever *demam*

field, empty space *lapangan*

fierce *galak*

fight over, to *merebut*

fight, to (physically) *bertengkar*

fill, to *isi, mengisi*

film *filem*

filter *saringan*

filter, to *saring, menyaring*

find, to *temu, temukan, menemukan, ketemu*

finger *jari*

fingernail *kuku*

finish off, to *habiskan, menghabiskan*

finish *selesaikan, menyelesaikan*

finished (completed) *selesai*

finished (no more) *habis*

fire *api*
fire someone, to *pecat, pecatkan*
first *pertama*
first, earlier, beforehand *dulu*
fish *ikan*
fish, to *pancing, memancing*
fit, to *pas*
fitting, suitable *cocok*
five *lima*
fix, to (a time, appointment) *menentukan*
fix, to (repair) *betulkan, membetulkan*
flag *bendéra*
flood *banjir*
floor *lantai*
flour *tepung*
flower *bunga, kembang*
flu *pilek, flu*
fluent *lancar*
flute *suling*
fly (insect) *lalat*
fly, to *terbang, menerbang*
follow along, to *ikut*
follow behind, to *menyusul*
following *berikut*
fond of, to be *sayang, menyayangi*
food *makanan*
foot *kaki*
for *untuk, demi, bagi*
forbid, to *melarang*
forbidden *dilarang*
force *daya*
force, to *paksa, memaksa*

foreign *asing*
foreigner *orang asing*
forest *hutan*
forget about, to *lupa, melupakan*
forget, to *lupa*
forgive, to *memaafkan, mengampuni*
forgiveness, mercy *ampun*
forgotten *terlupakan*
fork *garpu*
form (shape) *bentuk*
form (to fill out) *formulir*
fortress *bénténg*
four *empat*
free of charge *gratis, cuma-cuma*
free of restraints *bébas*
free, independent *merdéka*
freedom *kemérdekaan*
fresh *segar*
Friday *hari Jumat*
fried *goréng*
friend *kawan, teman*
friendly, outgoing *ramah*
from *dari*
front *depan, muka*
fruit *buah*
fry, to *goreng, menggoreng*
full *penuh*
full, eaten one's fill *kenyang*
fullfill, to *penuhi, memenuhi*
function, to work *jalan, berjalan*
funds, funding *dana*
fungus *jamur*
funny *lucu*

G

gamble *judi, berjudi*
garage (for repairs) *béngkél*
garage (for keeping a car) *garasi*
garbage *sampah*
garden *taman, kebun, halaman*
garlic *bawang putih*
gasoline *bénsin*
gasoline station *pompa bénsin*
gather, to *kumpul, berkumpul*
gender *jenis kelamin*
general, all-purpose *umum*
generally *pada umumnya*
gentle *lembut*
get, receive *dapat, mendapat, terima*
ghost *hantu*
gift *hadiah, kado*
girl *gadis, anak perempuan*
girlfriend *pacar*
give *beri, memberi; kasih*
glass (for drinking) *gelas*
glass (material) *kaca*
go *pergi, jalan*
go along, join in *ikut, mengikuti*
go around *keliling*
go back *balik, berbalik*
go down, get off *turun*
go for a walk *jalan-jalan*
go home *pulang*
go out, exit *keluar*
go up, climb *naik*
goal *tujuan*
goat *kambing*
God *Tuhan, Allah*

god *déwa*
goddess *déwi*
gold *emas, mas*
gone, finished *habis*
good *baik, bagus*
government *pemerintah*
grand, great *hebat*
grandchild *cucu*
grandfather *kakék*
grandmother *nénék*
grape *(buah) anggur*
grass *rumput*
grave *kuburan, makam*
gray *abu-abu*
great, formidable *hebat*
green *hijau*
green beans *buncis*
greet, to receive *sambut, menyambut*
greetings *salam*
grill, to *panggang, memanggang; bakar, membakar*
grow larger, to *berkembang, membesar*
grow, to (intransitive) *tumbuh, bertumbuh*
grow, plant *tanam, menanam*
guarantee *jaminan*
guarantee, to *jamin, menjamin*
guard, to *jaga, menjaga*
guess, to *kira*
guest *tamu*
guide, lead *antar, mengantar; pandu, memandu*
guidebook *buku panduan*

H

hair *rambut*

half *setengah, separuh*

hall *lorong; aula*

hand (also forearm) *tangan*

handicap *cacat*

handicraft *kerajinan*

handsome *cakap, ganteng*

hang, to *gantung, menggantung*

happen, occur *terjadi*

happened, what happened? *apa yang terjadi?*

happening, incident *kejadian*

happy *bahagia, gembira*

hard (difficult) *sukar, sulit, susah*

hard (solid) *keras*

hardworking, industrious *rajin*

harmonious *rukun*

hat *topi*

have been, ever *pernah*

have, own, belong to *punya*

he *dia*

head *kepala*

healthy *séhat*

hear, to *dengar*

heart *hati, jantung*

heavy *berat*

help, to *tolong, menolong; bantu, membantu*

her *dia*

here *sini, di sini*

hidden *tersembunyi*

hide, to *menyembunyikan*

high *tinggi*

hill *bukit*

him *dia*

hinder, to *menghambat*

hindrance *hambatan*

history *sejarah*

hit, strike *pukul, memukul*

hold back, to *tahan, bertahan*

hold onto, grasp *pegang, memegang*

hole *lubang*

holiday *liburan; hari libur*

holy *keramat, suci*

home, house *rumah*

honey *madu*

hope, to *harap, berharap*

horse *kuda*

hospital *rumah sakit*

hot (spicy) *pedas*

hot (temperature) *panas*

hot spring *mata air panas*

hour *jam*

house *rumah*

how are you? *apa kabar?*

how many? *berapa banyak?*

how much? *berapa?*

how? *bagaimana?*

human *manusia*

humane *manusiawi*

humorous *lucu*

hundred *seratus*

hungry *lapar*

hurt (injured) *luka, cedera*

hurt (to feel pain) *(berasa) sakit*

husband *suami*

hut, shack *pondok, gubuk*

I

I *saya*

ice *és*

if *kalau, jika*

imagine, to *bayangkan, membayangkan*

important *penting*

impossible *tidak mungkin*

impression *kesan*

impression, to make an *mengesankan, meninggalkan kesan*

in (time, years) *dalam (waktu)*

in order that, so that *agar, supaya*

in, at (space) *di*

included, including *termasuk*

increase, to *bertambah (banyak)*

indeed *memang!*

indigenous *asli*

influence *pengaruh*

influence, to *mempengaruhi*

influenza *flu*

inform, to *beritahu, memberitahukan*

information *keterangan, informasi*

information booth *penerangan*

inhale, to *isap, mengisap; hirup, menghirup*

inject, to *menyuntik, menyuntikkan*

injection *suntik, suntikan*

injury, injured *luka, cedera*

inside *dalam*

inside of *di dalam*

inspect, to *periksa, memeriksa*

instruct, send to do something *suruh, menyuruh*

insult *penghinaan*

insult someone, to *menghina*

insurance *asuransi*

intend, to *hendak, bermaksud*

intended for *ditujukan kepada, dimaksud untuk*

intention *maksud, niat*

interest (bank) *bunga*

interesting *menarik*

intersection *persimpangan, simpang jalan*

into *(ke) dalam*

invitation *(surat) undangan*

invite, to (ask along) *ajak, mengajak*

invite, to (formally) *undang, mengundang*

involve, to *melibatkan*

involved *terlibat*

iron *besi*

iron, to (clothing) *gosok, menggosok; setrika, menyetrika*

is *adalah, merupakan*

island *pulau, nusa*

it *ini, itu*

item *barang*

ivory *gading*

J

jail *penjara*

jam *selai*

January *bulan Januari*

jealous *cemburu*

job *pekerjaan, tugas*

join together, to *menyambung; gabung, bergabung*

join, go along *ikut, mengikuti*

journalist *wartawan*

Juli *bulan Juli*

jump, to *lompat, melompat*

June *bulan Juni*

jungle *hutan (rimba)*

just now *baru saja, baru tadi*

just, only *cuma, hanya, saja*

K

keep, to *simpan, menyimpan*

key *kunci*

kill, murder *membunuh*

kind, good (of persons) *baik (hati)*

kind, type *macam, jenis*

king *raja*

kiss *cium, mencium*

kitchen *dapur*

knife *pisau*

knock, to *ketuk, mengetuk*

know, to *tahu*

know, be acquainted with *kenal, mengenal*

knowledge *pengetahuan, ilmu*

L

ladle, dipper *gayung*

lady *wanita*

lake *danau, telaga*

lamb, mutton *daging kambing*

lamp *lampu*

land *tanah*

land, to (a plane) *mendarat*

lane (of a highway) *jalur, lajur*

lane (alleyway) *gang*

language *bahasa*

large *besar*

last night *tadi malam*

last *terakhir*

late at night *malam-malam*

late *terlambat, telat*

later *nanti*

laugh at, to *tertawakan, menertawakan*

laugh, to *tertawa, ketawa*

lavish, fancy *méwah*

laws, legislation *undang-undang, peraturan, hukum*

layer *lapisan*

lazy *malas*

lead (to be a leader) *memimpin*

lead (to guide someone somewhere) *antar, mengantar*

leader *pemimpin*

leaf *daun*

leather *kulit*

leave behind by accident *ketinggalan, tertinggal*

leave behind on purpose *tinggalkan, meninggalkan*

leave behind for safekeeping *titip, menitip*

leave, depart *pergi, berangkat, tinggal*

lecture *ceramah, kuliah*

lecturer (at university) *dosen*

left side *kiri*

leg (also foot) *kaki*

lend, to *pinjami, meminjami; pinjamkan, meminjamkan*

less *kurang*

lessen, reduce *mengurangi*

lesson *pelajaran, les*

let someone know, to *beritahu, kasih tahu*

let, allow *biar, biarkan, membiarkan*

letter *surat*

level (even, flat) *rata*

level (height) *ketinggian*

level (standard) *nilai, tingkat*

license (for driving) *SIM (surat izin mengemudi)*

license, permit *izin*

lie down, to *berbaring, tidur*

lie *bohong, berbohong*

life *nyawa; kehidupan*

lifetime *hidup*

lift *angkat, mengangkat*

light (bright) *terang*

light (lamp) *lampu*

light bulb *bola lampu, bohlam*

lightning *kilat*

lightweight *ringan, enteng*

like, as *seperti*

like, be pleased by *senang, suka*

line *garis*

line up, to *antri*

list *daftar*

listen *dengar, mendengar*

listen to *dengarkan, mendengarkan*

literature *sastra, kesusastraan*

little (not much) *sedikit*

little (small) *kecil*

live (stay in a place) *tinggal, berdiam*

live (be alive) *hidup*

liver *hati*

load *muatan*

load up, to *muat, memuat*

lock *kunci, gembok*

lock, to *mengunci*

locked *terkunci, dikunci*

lodge, small hotel *losmen, penginapan, hotel melati*

lonely *kesepian*

long (time) *lama*

long (length) *panjang*

look after, to *mengawasi, menjaga, mengasuh*

look for, to *cari, mencari*

look out! *awas!*

look, see *lihat, melihat*

lose money, to *rugi*

lose something, to *hilang, kehilangan*

lose, be defeated *kalah*

lost (of things) *hilang*

lost (to lose one's way) *menyasar, kesasar*

love *cinta, rasa sayang*

love, to *mencintai, menyayangi*

low *rendah*

loyal *setia*

luck *untung*

luggage *kopor, bagasi*

M

madam *nyonya*

magazine *majalah*

make, to *buat, membuat; bikin, membikin*

male *laki-laki*

man *pria, orang*

manufacture, to *buat, membuat, memproduksi*

many, much *banyak*

map *peta*

March *bulan Maret*

marijuana *ganja*

market *pasar*

market, to *pasarkan, memasarkan*

married *kawin, nikah*

marry, to *menikah*

mask *topéng*

massage *pijat*

massage, to *pijat, memijat*

mat *tikar, keset*

material, ingredient *bahan*

matter, issue *soal, hal*

mattress *kasur*

May *bulan Mei*

may *boléh*

maybe *mungkin, barangkali*

me *saya*

mean (to intend to) *bermaksud*

mean (cruel) *kejam, bengis*

mean, to *berarti*

meaning *arti, maksud*

measure, to *ukur, mengukur*

measurement *ukuran*

meat *daging*

meatball *bakso*

medicine *obat*

meet, to *bertemu, ketemu, jumpa, berjumpa*

meeting *pertemuan, rapat*

member *anggota*

memories *kenangan*

memory *ingatan*

mention, to *sebut, menyebut; sebutkan, menyebutkan*

mentioned *tersebut*

menu *daftar makanan*

mercy *ampun*

merely *cuma, hanya*

message *pesan*

metal *logam, besi*

method *cara*

meticulous *teliti*

middle, center *tengah*

middle, be in the middle of *sedang, lagi*

milk *susu*

million *juta*

mirror *kaca, cermin*

mix, mixed *campur*

modest, simple *sederhana*

moment (in a moment, just a moment) *sebentar*

moment (instant) *saat*

Monday *hari Sénin*

money *uang, duit*

monkey *monyet, kera*

month, moon *bulan*

monument *tugu*

moon, month *bulan*

more (comparative quality) *lebih*

more of (things) *lagi, lebih banyak*

morning *pagi*

mosque *mesjid*

mosquito *nyamuk*

mosquito netting *kelambu*

most (the most of) *paling banyak, terbanyak*

most (superlative) *paling*

most, at most *paling-paling*

mother *ibu*

mother-in-law *mertua*

motorcycle *motor, sepeda motor*

mountain *gunung*

mouse, rat *tikus*

moustache *kumis*

mouth *mulut*

move from one place to another *pindah, memindahkan*

move, to *gerak, bergerak*

movement, motion *gerakan*

movie theater *bioskop*

much, many *banyak*

mushroom *jamur*

must *harus*

mutton *daging kambing*

mutual, mutually *saling*

my, mine *saya (punya)*

N

nail (fingernail) *kuku*

nail (spike) *paku*

naked *telanjang*

name *nama*

narrow *sempit*

nation, country *negeri, negara*

nation, people *bangsa*

national *negara*

nationality *kebangsaan*

natural *alamiah*

nature *alam*

naughty *nakal*

nearby *dekat*

neat, orderly *rapi, teratur*

necessary, must *harus*

neck *léhér*

need *keperluan, kebutuhan*

need, to *perlu, butuh*

needle *jarum*

neighbor *tetangga*

nephew, niece *keponakan*

nest *sarang*

net *jaring*

network *jaringan*

never *tidak pernah*

new *baru*

news *kabar, berita*

newspaper *koran, surat kabar*

next (in line, sequence) *berikut*

next to *di samping, di sebelah*

niece, nephew *keponakan*

night *malam*

nightly *tiap malam*

nine *sembilan*

no, not (of nouns) *bukan*

no, not (of verbs and adjectives) *tidak*

noise *bunyi*

noisy *bising*

non-stop *langsung*

nonsense *omong kosong*

noodles *mie*

noon *tengah hari, jam dua belas siang*

normal *biasa*

normally *biasanya*

north *utara*

nose *hidung*

not *tidak, bukan*

not yet *belum*

note down, to *catat, mencatat*

notes *catatan*

novels *novel, roman*

November *bulan November*

now *sekarang*

nude *telanjang*

number *nomor*

O

o'clock *jam*

obey, to *turut, menurut; patuh, mematuhi*

occupation *pekerjaan*

ocean *laut, samudera*

October *bulan Oktober*

odor, bad smell *bau*

of, from *dari*

off, turn off *mematikan, menutup*

off, turned off *mati, tutup*

office *kantor*

official, formal *resmi*

officials (government) *pejabat*

often *sering*

oil *minyak*

old (of persons) *tua*

old (of things) *lama, tua, kuno*

older brother or sister *kakak*

on (of dates) *pada*

on time *pada waktunya, tepat waktu*

on, at *di*

on, turn on *hidupkan, menghidupkan; nyalakan, menyalakan; jalankan, menjalankan*

on, turned on *nyala, hidup, jalan*

once *sekali*

one *satu, se-*

one who, the one which *yang*

onion *bawang*

only *saja, cuma, hanya*

open *buka, terbuka*

open, to *buka, membuka*

opponent *lawan*

opportunity *kesempatan, peluang*

oppose, to *lawan, melawan*

opposed, in opposition *berlawanan, bertentangan*

or *atau*

orange, citrus *jeruk*

order (command) *perintah*

order (placed for food, goods) *pesanan*

order (sequence) *urutan*

order something, to *pesan, memesan*

order, to be in sequence *urut,*
berurutan

order, to command *perintah,*
memerintah; suruh, menyuruh

orderly, organized *teratur, rapi*

organize, arrange *atur, mengatur;*
urus, mengurus; selenggarakan,
menyelenggarakan

origin *asal, asal-usul*

original *asli*

originate, come from *berasal dari*

other *lain*

out *luar*

out, go out *keluar*

outside *luar, di luar*

over, finished *selesai*

over, to turn *balik*

overcast, cloudy *mendung*

overcome, to *mengatasi*

overseas *luar negeri*

overturned *terbalik*

own, to *milik, memiliki; punya,*
mempunyai

oyster *tiram*

P

pack, to *membungkus*

package *bungkus, paket*

paid *lunas*

painful *sakit*

paint *cat*

paint, to (a painting) *lukis,*
melukis

paint, to (houses, furniture) *cat,*
mengecat

painting *lukisan*

pair of, a *sepasang*

palace (Balinese) *puri*

palace (Javanese) *kraton*

palace *istana*

panorama *pemandangan*

pants *celana*

paper *kertas*

parcel *pakét, bungkus*

pardon me? what did you say?
kenapa?

parents *orang tua*

part *bagian*

participate, to *ikut (serta)*

particularly, especially *terutama,*
khususnya

party *pésta*

pass away, die, to *meninggal*
(dunia)

passenger *penumpang*

past (directional) *léwat, melalui*

past (time) *(masa) lalu*

patient (calm) *sabar*

patient (doctor's) *pasien*

pay, to *bayar, membayar*

payment *pembayaran*

peace *perdamaian*

peaceful *damai*

peak, summit *puncak*

peanut *kacang tanah*

peel, to *kupas, mengupas*

penetrate, to *tembus, menembus*

people *rakyat, orang*

pepper, black *merica, lada*

pepper, chili *lombok, cabe*

percent, percentage *persén*

performance *pertunjukan*

perhaps, maybe *mungkin, barangkali*

period (end of a sentence) *titik*

period (of time) *jangka waktu, masa*

permanent *tetap*

permit, license *izin*

permit, to allow *mengizinkan*

person *orang*

personality *watak*

pharmacy *apotik*

pick up, to (someone) *jemput, menjemput*

pick up, lift (something) *angkat, mengangkat*

pick, choose *pilih, memilih*

pickpocket *pencopét, copét*

pickpocket, to *copét, mencopét*

piece, portion, section *bagian*

pierce, penetrate, to *tembus, menembus*

pig, pork *babi*

pillow *bantal*

pineapple *nanas*

(what a) pity! *sayang!*

place *tempat*

place, put, to *taruh, menaruh; simpan, menyimpan*

plan *rencana*

plan, to *merencanakan*

plant *tanaman*

plant, to *tanam, menanam*

plate *piring*

play around, to *main-main*

play, to *main, bermain; memainkan*

please (go ahead) *silahkan, mari*

please (request for help) *tolong*

please (request for something) *minta*

pocket *kantong, saku*

point (in time) *saat*

point out, to *menunjuk*

point, dot *titik*

poison *racun*

poisonous *beracun*

police *polisi*

pond *kolam*

pool *kolam (renang)*

poor *miskin*

pork, pig *babi*

porpoise *lumba-lumba*

possible *mungkin, bisa, boleh*

post, column *tiang*

postpone, to *tunda, menunda*

postponed, delayed *tertunda, ditunda*

potato *kentang*

pour, to *tuangkan, menuangkan*

power *kuasa, kekuasaan, kekuatan*

powerful *berkuasa, kuat*

practice *latihan*

practice, to *berlatih, melatih, latihan*

prawn *udang*

pray, to *berdoa, sembahyang, sholat*

prayer *doa*

pregnant *hamil*

prejudice *prasangka*

prepare, to make ready *bersiap-siap, siapkan, menyiapkan*

prepared, ready *siap*

prescription *resép*

present moment, at the *pada saat ini, sekarang*

presently, nowadays *sekarang, kini*

press, journalism *pers*

press, to *tekan, menekan*

pressure *tekanan*

pretty (of places, things) *indah, asri*

pretty (of women) *cantik*

pretty, very *cukup, agak*

price *harga*

priest *pendéta, pastor*

print *cétak*

private *pribadi*

probably *kemungkinan besar, barangkali*

problem *masalah*

produce *buat, membuat; menghasilkan, memproduksikan*

profit, luck *untung*

program, schedule *acara*

promise, to *janji, berjanji*

proof *bukti*

prove, to *membuktikan*

public *umum*

publish, to *menerbitkan*

pull, to *tarik, menarik*

pump *pompa*

pure *murni*

purse *dompet*

push, to *dorong, mendorong*

put into, inside *masukkan, memasukkan*

put together, to *pasang, memasang*

put, to place *taruh, menaruh; simpan, menyimpan*

Q

quarter *seperempat*

queen *ratu*

question *pertanyaan*

question, to *pertanyakan, mempertanyakan; tanyai, menanyai*

queue (up) *antre*

quiet *sepi*

quite *agak*

R

rain (to) *hujan*

raise, lift, to *angkat, mengangkat*

rank, station in life *pangkat*

ranking *urutan*

rare (scarce) *langka*

rare (uncooked) *mentah*

rarely, seldom *jarang*

rat *tikus*

rate of exchange (for foreign currency) *kurs*

rate, tariff *tarip, ongkos*

rather *agak*

rather than *daripada, melainkan*

raw, uncooked, rare *mentah*

ray *sinar*

reach *sampai, mencapai*

react, to *menanggapi*

reaction, response *tanggapan*

read *baca, membaca*

ready *siap*

ready, to get *bersiap*

ready, to make *siapkan, menyiapkan; persiapkan, mempersiapkan*

realize, be aware of *sadari, menyadari*

really *sungguh, benar-benar*

rear, tail *buntut, ekor*

receive *terima, menerima*

recipe *resép*

recognize, to *kenal, mengenal*

recovered, cured *sembuh*

red *mérah*

reduce, to *kurangi, mengurangi*

refined *halus*

reflect, to *mencerminkan*

refuse, to *tolak, menolak*

regarding *terhadap, mengenai*

region *daerah*

register, to *daftar, mendaftar*

registered post *pos tercatat*

registered *terdaftar*

regret, to *menyesal*

regular, normal *biasa*

relax *santai, bersantai*

release, to *lepaskan, melepaskan*

released *terlepas, dilepaskan*

religion *agama*

remainder, leftover *sisa*

remains (historical) *peninggalan*

remember, to *ingat*

remind, to *mengingatkan*

rent, to *séwa, menyéwa*

rent out, to *séwakan, menyéwakan*

repair, to *membetulkan, memperbaiki*

repaired *betul, baik*

repeat, to *ulang, mengulangi*

reply, response *balasan, jawaban*

reply, to (in writing or deeds) *membalas*

reply, to (verbally) *menjawab*

report *laporan*

report, to *lapor, melapor*

request, to (formally) *mohon, memohon*

request, to (informally) *minta*

research *penelitian, riset*

research, to *selidiki, menyelidiki*

reservation *reservasi, pesanan*

reserve, nature *cagar alam*

reserve, to ask for in advance *pesan dulu*

resident, inhabitant *penduduk, penghuni*

resolve, to (a problem) *mengatasi, membereskan*

respect *hormat*

respect, to *menghormati*

respond, react *menanggapi*

response, reaction *tanggapan*

responsibility *tanggung jawab*

responsible, to be *bertanggung jawab*

rest, relax *istirahat, beristirahat*

restrain, to *tahan, menahan*

restroom *kamar kecil, toilet, WC*

result *akibat, hasil*

resulting from, as a result of
akibatnya, dampaknya

return home, to *pulang*

return (to give back)
mengembalikan

return (go back) *kembali, balik*

reverse, back up *mundur*

reversed, backwards *terbalik*

rice (cooked) *nasi*

rice (plant) *padi*

rice (uncooked grains) *beras*

rice paddy, ricefield *sawah*

rich *kaya*

rid, get rid of *membuang,
menghilangkan*

ride, mount, climb *naik*

right, correct *betul, benar*

right-hand side *kanan*

rights *hak*

ring *cincin*

ripe *matang, masak*

river *kali, sungai*

road *jalan*

roast, grill *panggang, bakar*

roasted, grilled, toasted *bakar,
panggang*

role *peranan*

room *kamar, ruangan*

root *akar*

rope *tali*

rotten *busuk*

rough *kasar*

run, to *lari*

S

sacred *keramat, suci*

sacrifice *korban*

sacrifice, to *mengorbankan*

sad *sedih*

safe *selamat*

sail *layar*

sail, to *berlayar*

salary *gaji*

sale (at reduced prices) *obral*

sales *penjualan*

salt *garam*

salty *asin*

same *sama*

sample *contoh*

sand *pasir*

satisfied *puas*

satisfy, to *memuaskan*

Saturday *hari Sabtu*

sauce *saus, kecap*

sauce (chilli) *sambal*

save money, to *menghemat*

save, keep, to *simpan, menyimpan*

say, to *berkata, mengatakan*

scarce *langka*

schedule *jadwal*

school *sekolah*

science *ilmu pengetahuan alam
(IPA), sains*

scissors *gunting*

scrub, to *gosok, menggosok*

sculpt, to *pahat, memahat*

sculpture *patung*

sea *laut*

search for, to *cari, mencari*

season *musim*

seat *tempat duduk, kursi*

second *kedua*

secret *rahasia*

secret, to keep a *rahasiakan, merahasiakan*

secretary *sékretaris*

secure, safe *aman, selamat*

see, to (*also* observe, visit) *lihat, melihat*

seed *biji*

seek, to *cari, mencari*

select, to *pilih, memilih*

self *diri, sendiri*

sell, to *jual, menjual*

send, to *kirim, mengirim*

sentence *kalimat*

separate, to *pisah, memisahkan*

September *bulan September*

sequence, order *urutan*

serious (not funny) *serius*

serious, severe (of problems, illnesses, etc.) *parah*

servant *pelayan, pembantu*

serve, to *melayani*

service *pelayanan, service*

seven *tujuh*

severe (of problems, illnesses, etc.) *parah*

sew, to *jahit, menjahit*

sex, gender *kelamin*

shack *pondok, gubuk*

shadow *bayang, bayangan*

shadow play *wayang kulit*

shake, to (intransitive) *goyang, bergoyang*

shake something, to (transitive) *kocok, mengocok; menggoyangkan*

shall, will *akan*

shape *bentuk*

shape, to form *membentuk*

sharp *tajam*

shatter, to *pecahkan, memecahkan*

shattered *pecah*

shave, to *cukur, mencukur*

she *dia*

sheep *domba*

ship *kapal*

shirt *baju, kemeja*

shit *bérak*

shoes *sepatu*

shop, store *toko*

shop, go shopping, to *belanja, berbelanja*

short (concise) *ringkas, péndék*

short (not tall) *péndék*

short time, a moment *sebentar*

shoulder *bahu, pundak*

shout, to *teriak, berteriak*

show, broadcast *siaran*

show, live performance *pertunjukan*

show, to *menunjukkan, memperlihatkan*

shrimp, prawn *udang*

shut *tutup, menutupi*

sick *sakit*

side *samping*

sign, symbol *syarat*

sign, to *tandatangani, menandatangani*

signature *tanda tangan*

signboard *papan, reklame, baliho*

silent, quiet *diam; sepi*

silk *sutera*

silver *pérak*

simple (easy) *gampang, mudah*

simple (uncomplicated, modest) *sederhana*

since *sejak*

sinews *urat*

sing, to *nyanyi, bernyani*

sir *tuan*

sister *saudara perempuan, adik/ kakak perempuan*

sister-in-law *ipar*

sit down, to *duduk*

six *enam*

sixteen *enam belas*

sixty *enam puluh*

size *ukuran, kebesaran*

skewer *tusuk*

skin *kulit*

sky *langit*

sleep, to *tidur*

sleepy *ngantuk, mengantuk*

slow *pelan, lambat*

slowly *pelan-pelan*

small *kecil*

smart *pandai, pintar*

smell, bad odor *bau*

smell, to *cium, mencium*

smile, to *senyum, tersenyum*

smoke *asap*

smoke, to (tobacco) *merokok*

smooth (to go smoothly) *lancar*

smooth (of surfaces) *rata, mulus*

smuggle, to *selundupkan, menyelundupkan*

snake *ular*

snow *salju*

snowpeas *kacang kapri*

so that *agar, supaya*

so, very *begitu*

soap *sabun*

socks *kaus kaki*

soft *empuk, lunak*

sold out *habis*

sold *terjual, laku*

sole, only *tunggal, satu-satunya*

solve, to (a problem) *menyelesaikan, membéréskan*

solved, resolved *bérés, selesai*

some *beberapa*

sometimes *kadang-kadang*

son *anak (laki-laki)*

son-in-law *menantu*

song *lagu*

soon *segera*

sorry, to feel regretful *menyesal*

sorry! *maaf!*

soul *jiwa*

sound *bunyi*

soup (clear) *sop, kuah*

soup (spicy stew) *soto*

sour *asam, kecut*

source *sumber*

south *selatan*

soy sauce (salty) *kecap asin*

soy sauce (sweet) *kecap manis*

space *tempat*

spacious *luas, lapang*

speak, to *bicara, berkata*

special *khusus, istiméwa*

speech *pidato*

speed *(laju) kecepatan*

spend, to *keluarkan, mengeluarkan*

spices *rempah-rempah*

spinach *bayam, kangkung*

spirit *semangat, nyawa*

spoiled (does not work) *rusak*

spoiled (of food) *busuk*

spoon *séndok*

spray, to *semprot, menyemprot*

spring *mata air, sumber*

square (shape) *persegi*

square, town square *alun-alun*

squid *cumi-cumi, sotong*

stamp (ink) *cap*

stamp (postage) *perangka*

stand up, to *berdiri*

star *bintang*

start, to *mulai, memulai*

startled *terkejut*

startling *mengejutkan*

statue *patung*

stay overnight, to *menginap, bermalam*

stay, to *tinggal, berdiam*

steal, to *curi, mencuri*

steam *uap*

steamed *kukus*

steel *baja*

step *langkah*

steps, stairs *tangga*

stick out, to *menonjol*

stick, pole *batang*

stick to, to *melekat, menémpél*

sticky *lengket*

stiff *kaku*

still *masih*

stink, to *bau, berbau*

stomach, belly *perut*

stone *batu*

stop by, to pay a visit *mampir*

stop, to *berhenti, stop*

store *toko*

store, to *simpan, menyimpan*

story (of a building) *lantai, tingkat*

story (tale) *cerita, dongeng*

straight (not crooked) *lurus*

straight ahead *terus, lurus*

strait *selat*

street *jalan*

strength *kekuatan*

strict *ketat*

strike, to go on *mogok kerja*

strike, hit *pukul, memukul*

string *tali*

strong *kuat*

struck, hit *kena, terpukul*

stubborn, determined *nekad, ngotot*

study, learn *belajar*

stupid *bodoh*

style *gaya*

submerged, drowned *tenggelam*

succeed, to *berhasil*

success *keberhasilan*

suddenly *tiba-tiba*

suffer, to *sengsara*

suffering *kesengsaraan*

sugar *gula*

sugarcane *tebu*

suggest *mengusulkan, menyarankan*

suggestion *usul, saran*

suitable, fitting, compatible *cocok*

suitcase *koper*

summit, peak *puncak*

sun *matahari*

Sunday *hari Minggu/Ahad*

sunlight *sinar matahari*

supermarket *(toko) swalayan, supermarket*

suppose, to *kira, mengira*

sure *pasti, yakin*

surf *buih, busa*

surface *permukaan*

surprised *héran*

surprising *menghérankan*

suspect, to *mencuriga, menduga, menyangka*

suspicion *kecurigaan*

sweat *keringat*

sweep, to *sapu, menyapu*

sweet *manis*

swim, to *berenang*

swimming pool *kolam renang*

swimming suit *pakaian renang*

swing, to *goyang, bergoyang*

switch on, turn on *pasang, memasang; nyalakan, menyalakan; hidupkan, menghidupkan*

switch, change *ganti, mengganti*

T

t-shirt *kaus*

table *méja*

tail *ékor, buntut*

take *ambil, mengambil*

tall *tinggi*

taste *rasa*

tasty *énak*

tea *téh*

teach, to *ajar, mengajar*

teacher *guru, pengajar*

team *regu*

teen *remaja*

teeth *gigi*

tell, to (a story) *menceritakan*

tell, to (let know) *beritahu, kasih tahu*

temple (ancient) *candi*

temple (Balinese-Hindu) *pura*

temple (Chinese) *klénténg*

temple (Indian) *kuil*

temporary, temporarily *sementara*

ten *sepuluh*

tendon *urat*

tens of, multiples of ten *puluhan*

tense *tegang*

test *ujian*

test, to *uji, menguji*

than *daripada*

thank you *terima kasih*

that (introducing a quotation or clause) *bahwa*

that, those *itu*

that, which, the one who *yang*

theater, cinema *bioskop*

their, theirs *meréka punya*

then *lalu, kemudian, lantas*

there *di sana, di situ*

they, them *meréka*

thick (of liquids) *kental*

thick (of things) *tebal*

thief *pencuri, maling*

thin (of liquids) *encer*

thin (of persons) *kurus*

thing *barang, benda*

think, to *pikir, berpikir*

third *ketiga*

thirsty *haus*

thirteen *tiga belas*

this, these *ini*

thoughts *pikiran*

thousand *ribu*

thread *benang*

three *tiga*

through, past *lewat, melalui*

throw out, throw away, to *buang, membuang*

thunder *gemuruh, geluduk*

Thursday *hari Kamis*

thus, so *begini, begitu, demikian*

ticket *karcis, tiket*

ticket window *loket*

tie, necktie *dasi*

tie, to *ikat, mengikat*

tiger *macan, harimau*

time to time, once in a while *sewaktu-waktu, sekali-sekali*

time *waktu, masa*

times (x) *kali*

tip (end) *ujung*

tip (gratuity) *hadiah, persenan, uang rokok*

tired (sleepy) *ngantuk, mengantuk*

tired (worn out) *capai*

title (of books, films) *judul*

title (of persons) *gelar*

to, toward (a person) *kepada*

to, toward (a place) *ke*

today *hari ini*

together *bersama-sama, sekalian*

toilet *kamar kecil*

tomato *tomat*

tomorrow *bésok*

tongue *lidah*

tonight *nanti malam*

too (also) *juga*

too (excessive) *terlalu*

too bad! *sayang!*

too much *terlalu banyak*

tool, utensil, instrument *alat*

tooth *gigi*

top *atas*

touch, to *sentuh, menyentuh*

towards *menuju*

towel *handuk*

tower *menara*

town *kota*

trade, business *perdagangan, niaga, bisnis*
trade, to exchange *tukar, menukar*
train *keréta api*
train station *setasiun (keréta api)*
tree *pohon*
tribe *suku*
trouble *kesusahan, kesulitan*
trouble, to *mengganggu, merépotkan*
troublesome *menyusahkan, merépotkan*
true *benar, betul*
truly *sungguh-sungguh*
try *coba, mencoba*
Tuesday *hari Selasa*
turn around *putar, berputar*
turn off, to *mematikan*
turn on, to *nyalakan, menyalakan; pasang, memasang; hidupkan, menghidupkan*
turn, make a turn *bélok, membélok*
turtle (land) *kura-kura*
turtle (sea) *penyu*
twelve *dua belas*
twenty *dua puluh*
two *dua*
type, sort *macam, jenis*

U

ugly *jelek*
umbrella *payung*
uncle *paman, om*
uncooked *mentah*

under *di bawah*
understand, to *mengerti*
underwear *pakaian dalam*
university *universitas*
unneccessary *tidak usah, tidak perlu*
unripe, young *muda*
until *sampai*
upside down *terbalik*
upstairs *di (atas)*
urge, to push for *mendesak*
urinate, to *kencing, buang air kecil*
use, to *pakai, memakai; gunakan, menggunakan*
useful, to be *berguna*
useless *tidak berguna, sia-sia*
usual *biasa*
usually *biasanya, pada umumnya*

V

vaccination *suntikan, vaksinasi, imunisasi*
valid *berlaku*
value *harga*
value, to *hargai, menghargai*
vegetable *sayur*
vegetables *sayur-sayuran*
very, extremely *sangat, sekali*
via *melalui, léwat*
view, panorama *pemandangan*
view, to look at *memandang, melihat*
village *kampung, désa*
vinegar *cuka*
visit *kunjungan*

visit, to pay a *berkunjung, mengunjungi*

voice *suara*

volcano *gunung api*

vomit, to *muntah*

W

wages *gaji, upah*

wait for, to *tunggu, menunggu; nantikan, menantikan*

waiter, waitress *pelayan*

wake someone up *membangunkan*

wake up *bangun*

walk *jalan, berjalan*

wall *témbok, dinding*

wallet *dompét*

want, to *ingin*

war, battle *perang, peperangan*

war, to make *berperang*

warm *hangat*

warn, to *memberi teguran, mengingatkan*

warning *teguran, peringatan*

wash *cuci, mencuci; mandi, memandikan*

watch (wristwatch) *jam (tangan)*

watch over, guard *mengawasi, menjaga*

watch, to (a show or movie) *menonton*

watch, look, see *lihat, melihat*

water *air*

water buffalo *kerbau*

waterfall *air terjun*

watermelon *semangka*

wave *ombak*

wax *lilin*

way of, by *melalui*

way, method *cara*

we (excludes the one addressed) *kami*

we (includes the one addressed) *kita*

weak *lemah*

weapon *senjata*

wear, to *pakai, memakai*

weary *capai, lelah*

weather *cuaca*

weave, to *tenun, menenun*

weaving *tenunan*

Wednesday *hari Rabu*

week *minggu*

weekly *tiap minggu*

weigh, to *timbang, menimbang*

weight *berat*

welcome, to *sambut, menyambut*

welcome, you're welcome! *sama-sama! kembali!*

well (for water) *sumur*

well, good *baik*

well-cooked, ripe, well-done *matang*

west *barat*

westerner *orang barat*

wet *basah*

what *apa*

wheel *roda*

when, at the time *waktu, ketika*

when? *kapan?*

where to? *ke mana?*

where? *mana?*

while ago *tadi*

while, awhile *sebentar*

while, during *sambil*

white *putih*

who? *siapa?*

whole, all of *seluruh*

whole, to be complete *utuh*

why? *kenapa?*

wicked *jahat*

wide, width *lebar*

widow *janda*

wife *isteri*

will, shall *akan*

win, to *menang*

wind, breeze *angin*

window *jendela*

wine *anggur*

wing *sayap*

winner *pemenang, juara (satu)*

wire *kawat*

with *dengan, bersama, beserta*

without *tanpa*

witness *saksi*

witness, to *saksikan, menyaksikan*

woman *perempuan*

wood *kayu*

word *kata*

work on *mengerjakan*

work, occupation *pekerjaan*

work, to function *jalan, berjalan, hidup*

work, to *kerja, bekerja*

world *dunia*

worry, to *kuatir*

wrap, to *membungkus*

write, to *tulis, menulis; karang, mengarang*

writer *pengarang*

wrong, false *salah*

Y

yawn *menguap*

year *tahun*

yell, to *teriak, berteriak*

yellow *kuning*

yes *ya*

yesterday *kemarin*

yet, not yet *belum*

you (familiar) *engkau, kamu;* (formal) *anda, saudara*

you (female) *ibu*

you (male) *bapak*

you're welcome! *kembali, sama-sam*a

young, unripe *muda*

younger brother or sister *adik (laki-laki/perempuan)*

youth (state of being young) *masa muda*

youth (young person) *remaja*

Z

zero *nol, kosong*

zoo *kebun binatang*

Indonesian–English Dictionary

The following is a list of words commonly used in colloquial, everyday speech. Words borrowed directly from English have generally been omitted since they will be readily understood by English speakers.

Verbs are normally listed under their root forms, without prefixes or suffixes (if in brackets, the root form does not exist alone). The most important prefixed and suffixed forms are then given. For more information on verbal affixes and derived forms, see Appendix A.

Nouns derived from simple roots have been listed alphabetically with their respective prefixes and suffixes attached, rather than being listed under the root word. This means you don't have to know what the root is, but can simply look up the affixed form.

A

abang older brother

abu-abu gray

acara program

ada be, have, exist

adat custom, tradition, culture

adik younger brother or sister

adu, mengadu to complain; *pengaduan* complaint

agak rather

agama religion; *beragama* to have a religion

agar in order that, so that

agén agent

ahli expert

air water

air matang boiled water

air minum drinking water

air panas hot water, hot spring

air terjun waterfall

ajak, mengajak to ask along, invite

ajar, mengajar to teach

akan shall, will

akar root

akhir last, end; *terakhir* the last

akibat result

aku I (informal)

alam nature

alamat address

alat tool, utensil, instrument

alun-alun town square (in Java)

alus refined

aman secure, safe

ambil, mengambil to take

ampun forgiveness, mercy

anak child

anak laki-laki son

anak perempuan daughter

anda you (formal)

anggota member

anggur grape, wine

angin wind

angkat, mengangkat to lift, raise up

angkot (angkutan kota) public minibus

anjing dog

antar, mengantar to guide, lead; *pengantar* guide

antara among, between

antré stand in line, queue up; *antréan* queue

apa? what?

apa kabar? how are you?

apel apple

api fire

apotik pharmacy

arah direction

arti; berarti meaning; to mean

asal; berasal origin; to originate

asam sour

asap smoke

asin salty

asing foreign

asli indigenous, original

atas above, upstairs

atau or

atur, mengatur to arrange, organize

awas! be careful! look out!

ayah father

ayam chicken

ayo come on, let's go

B

babi pork

baca, membaca to read; *bacaan* reading material

badan body

bagaimana? how?

bagasi baggage

bagi divide, share; *bagian* part

bagus good

bahagia happy

bahan material, ingredient

bahasa language; *bahasa Indonesia* Indonesian; *bahasa Inggris* English

bahaya danger; *berbahaya* dangerous

bahu shoulder

bahwa that (introduces a clause)

baik good; *memperbaiki* to fix, improve; *perbaikan* repairs

bajaj (pronounced "bajai") three-wheeled minicar, tuk-tuk

baju shirt

bakar, membakar to burn; roasted, toasted (of food)

bakso meatball

balas, membalas to answer (a letter)

balasan a reply

balik turn over, go back; *terbalik* reversed, backwards

banding, dibanding compared to

bandingkan, membandingkan to compare to

bangsa race, people; *kebangsaan* nationality

bangun, membangun awaken;
  to build
banjir flooded; flood
bantal pillow
bantu, membantu to help;
  pembantu servant
banyak many, much
bapak father
barang thing, item
barangkali maybe, perhaps
barat west
baru new, just now
basah wet
batal, membatalkan to cancel
batang stick, pole
batas edge, boundary
batu stone
batuk cough
bau smell, odor (bad)
bayi baby
bawa, membawa to carry
bawah below, downstairs
bawang onion
bawang putih garlic
bayam spinach
bayang shadow
bayangkan, membayangkan to
  imagine
bayar, membayar to pay
béa cukai customs duty
bébas free, unrestrained
bébék duck
beberapa some
bécak pedicab
béda, berbéda to differ; to be
  different; *perbédaan* difference

begini thus, so, like this
begitu thus, so, like that
béha bra, brassiere
bekerja to work
belajar to study
belakang behind
belanja shop, go shopping
belas teen; *belasan* dozens;
  sebelas eleven
beli, membeli to buy
bélok to turn; *bélokan* turn
belum not yet; *sebelum* before
bemo public minibus
benang thread
benar true
bendéra flag
béngkél garage (for repairs)
bénténg fort
bentuk, berbentuk shape; shaped
bérak shit, defecate
berangkat to depart
berani brave
berapa? how many? how
  much?
berarti to mean
beras (uncooked) rice
berasal to originate
berat heavy
berbéda to differ, be different;
  perbédaan difference
berbicara to speak
berbuat to do, make
berbunyi to make noise
bercakap to speak;
  percakapan conversation
bercerita to tell a story

berdiri to stand (up)

berenang to swim

berencana to plan; planned

bérés solved, arranged, okay

béréskan, membéréskan to solve, arrange

bergerak to move

berguna to be useful

berharap to hope

berhasil to succeed

berhenti to stop; *perhentian* (bus) stop

beri, memberi to give

berikut next, following; *berikutnya* the next, the following

berita news

berjanji to promise

berjudi to gamble

berjumpa to meet

berkembang to develop, expand

berkunjung to visit; *kunjungan* visit

berlaku to be valid

berlayar to sail

bermain to play; *permainan* game

bernyanyi to sing

berpikir to think

bersih clean; *kebersihan* hygiene, cleanliness

bersihkan, membersihkan to clean

bertentangan to be opposed, at odds

berubah to change; *perubahan* change

besar big

beserta together with

besi metal, iron

bésok tomorrow

betul true, correct; *kebetulan* accidentally, by chance

betulkan, membetulkan to correct, fix

biar! forget about it!

biarkan, membiarkan to allow, let alone, leave be

biasa usual, regular, normal; *kebiasaan* habit; custom

bibi aunt

bicara, berbicara to speak

biji seed

bikin, membikin to do, make; *bikinan* product of

bilang say, count

binatang animal

bintang star

bioskop movie theater, cinema

biru blue

bis bus

bisa can, be able to

blus blouse

bodoh stupid

bola ball

boléh be allowed to, may

bon bill

bongkar break apart, unpack, take apart

borong, memborong to buy up

bosan bored; *membosankan* boring

buah fruit, piece

buang, membuang to throw away

buang air besar defecate

buang air kecil urinate

buat for; do, make; *berbuat* to do; *membuat* to make; *buatan* product of

bubur porridge

budaya, kebudayaan culture

buka, membuka open

bukan not, none

bukit hill

bukti proof

buktikan, membuktikan to prove

buku book

bulan month, moon

bumi the earth

buncis green beans

bunga flower

bungkus wrap; a package

buntut rear, tail

bunuh, membunuh to kill; *pembunuhan* murder, killing

bunyi a sound; to sound; *berbunyi* to make noise

burung bird

busuk rotten

C

cabai, cabé chili pepper

cabang branch

cacat disabled, impaired

cagar alam nature reserve

cahaya rays

caisim Chinese cabbage

cakap, cakep handsome

campur mixed; mix

candi ancient temple

cangkir cup

cantik beautiful

cap brand

capai, mencapai to reach, attain

capai, capék tired, weary; *kecapékan* tired; fatigue

cara way

cari, mencari to look for

cat paint

catat, mencatat to note down

catatan notes

catur chess

celaka bad luck; *kecelakaan* an accident

celana pants; *celana dalam* underpants

cemburu jealous

cepat fast; *kecepatan* speed

cerah clear (of weather)

cerai divorced

cerita story; *bercerita* to tell a story; *menceritakan* to tell (something)

cermin mirror; *mencerminkan* to reflect

cétak, mencétak to print

cincin ring (jewelry)

cinta love; *mencintai* to love

cita-cita goal, ideal

cium, mencium to kiss, smell

coba, mencoba to try (on)

cocok fit, suit, match

cokelat brown; chocolate

contoh sample, example
copét pickpocket
cuaca weather
cuci, mencuci to wash
cuka vinegar
cukup enough
cukur shave
cuma merely
cumi-cumi squid
curi, mencuri to steal; *pencuri* thief; *pencurian* theft
curiga to suspect

D

dada chest
daérah region, district
daftar register; list; *pendaftaran* registration
dagang business; *pedagang* trader, seller
daging meat
dalam inside
dalang puppeteer
damai peaceful
dampingi, mendampingi to accompany
dan and
danau lake
dapat get, can; *mendapat* to get, reach, receive
dapur kitchen
darah blood
darat land; *mendarat* to land
dari from, of
daripada than

darurat emergency
dasar base, basis
datang arrive, come; *kedatangan* arrival
daun leaf
daya force
debu dust
dekat near
dekati, mendekati to approach
delapan eight
demam fever
demi for, in the name of
déndéng meat jerky
dengan with
dengar, mendengar to hear; *dengarkan, mendengarkan* to listen to
depan front, next
derajat degrees
désa village
desak to urge, push
déwa god (Hindu or eastern religions)
di in, at, on; *di atas* on top of, above, upstairs; *di bawal* below, underneath, downstairs
di- the passive form of verbs
di mana? where?
dia he, she, it; him, her
diam silent
dilarang to be forbidden
dinas (government) service
dingin cold
diri self; *berdiri* (to) stand (up)
dirikan, mendirikan to build, establish

doa prayer
dokar cart
dompét wallet
dorong, mendorong to push
dosén university lecturer
dua two; *kedua* second
dua belas twelve
dua puluh twenty
duduk sit down
duit money (slang)
dulu first, beforehand
dunia world
duta besar ambassador

E

ékor tail
emas gold
empat four; *perempatan* crossroads
énak tasty
enam six
éncér runny (of liquids)
engkau you
erat close, tight
és ice; *és krim* ice cream
ésok hari the following day

G

gabung join together
gading ivory
gadis girl
gado-gado vegetable salad with peanut sauce
gagah strong, dashing

gagal fail
gajah elephant
gaji wages, salary
galak fierce
gambar picture, drawing, image
gambarkan, menggambarkan to draw, describe
gampang easy
gang lane, alley
ganggu, mengganggu to disturb, annoy
gangguan disturbance
ganja marijuana
ganti, menggantikan to change, replace
gantung hang
garam salt
garis line
garpu fork
gaya style
gayung ladle, dipper (for washing)
gedung building
gelang bracelet, bangle
gelanggang arena
gelap dark
gelar title, degree
gelas (drinking) glass
gema echo
gemar like, be a fan of
gembira happy, rejoicing
gemuk fat
gerak, bergerak to move; *gerakan* movement
geréja church
giat active

gigi tooth, teeth

gila crazy

golongan class, category

goréng fried; *goréngan* fried food

gosok scrub, brush; iron

goyang swing, shake; unstable

gua cave

gugur wilt, fall (of leaves)

gula sugar

gulai spicy soup

guling rotate; bolster pillow

guna use, for; *berguna* to be useful

gunakan, menggunakan to (make) use (of)

gunting scissors

gunung mountain

gunung api volcano

guru teacher

H

habis gone, finished

habiskan, menghabiskan to finish off

hadapi, menghadapi to face, confront

hadiah gift

hadir attend

hadirin attendees

hak rights

hak asasi manusia (HAM) human rights

halte bus stop

halus refined

hambat, menghambat to hinder

hambatan hindrance

hamil pregnant

hampir almost

hancur destroyed

hancurkan, menghancurkan to destroy

handuk towel

hangat warm

hantu ghost

hanya only

harap, berharap to hope; *harapan* hope

harapkan, mengharapkan to expect, hope for

harga price, cost

hari day (of the week)

hari ini today

harus must

hasil result; *berhasil* to succeed

hasilkan, menghasilkan to produce

hati heart, liver

hati-hati! be careful!

haus thirsty

hébat great

hémat economical

hendak intend to

henti, berhenti to stop; *perhentian* (bus) stop

héran surprised

hidung nose

hidup live, living

hijau green

hilang lose; lost

hilangkan, menghilangkan to get rid of

hitam black

hitung count

hormat respect

hubungan contacts

hubungi, menghubungi to contact

hujan rain, rainy

hukum law

hutan forest, jungle

I

ibu mother

ikan fish

ikat tie; handwoven textiles

iklim climate

ikut, mengikuti to follow or go along, accompany; *berikut* following

ilmu science, knowledge

imbang equal

indah beautiful (of things, places)

ingat to remember

ingatkan, mengingatkan to remind

ini this

intan diamond

interlokal long distance telephone

inti essence, core

ipar brother/sister-in-law

iri envious

isap, mengisap to inhale, suck

isi, mengisi to fill

isteri wife

istiméwa special

istirahat rest; *beristirahat* to (take a) rest

itu that

izin permit, license

J

jadi, menjadi to become, happen

jadwal schedule

jaga, menjaga to guard

jagung corn

jahat wicked

jahit, menjahit to sew

jalan walk, go, function; street or road

jalan-jalan go out, go walking

jalur lane (of a highway)

jam hour, o'clock

jamin, menjamin to guarantee, assure

jaminan guarantee, assurance

jamur fungus, mushrooms

janda widow

jangan don't, do not!

jangka period (of time)

janji, berjanji to promise; *perjanjian* agreement; appointment

jantung heart

jarak distance

jarang rarely

jari finger(s)

jaring net

jarum needle

jasa service

jatuh fall

jauh far

jawab, menjawab to answer, reply

jawaban an answer

jelas clear

jelaskan, menjelaskan to clarify, explain

jelék bad, ugly

jembatan bridge

jemput, menjemput to pick someone up

jemur dry out; *jemuran* washing hung out to dry

jendéla window

jenis type

jeruk orange, citrus fruit

jika if, when

jiwa soul

jual, menjual to sell

juara champion

judi, berjudi to gamble

judul title of book, article

juga also

Jumat Friday

jumlah amount, total

jumpa, berjumpa to meet

jurusan direction

juta million

K

kabar, khabar news

kaca (sheet) glass; mirror

kacamata glasses, spectacles

kacang bean, peanut

kacau confused, messy

kadang-kadang sometimes

kain cloth

kakak older brother or sister

kakék grandfather

kaki leg, foot

kaku stiff

kalah lose, be defeated

kalahkan, mengalahkan to defeat

kalau if, when, what about?, how about?

kali times, occurrences; river

kalimat sentence

kamar room

kamar kecil toilet, restroom

kamar mandi bathroom

kamar tidur bedroom

kambing lamb, mutton, goat, sheep

kami we (excluding the person addressed)

Kamis Thursday

kampung village; countryside

kamu you

kamus dictionary

kanan right

kangkung a kind of water spinach

kantong, kantung pocket

kantor office

kapal ship

kapan? when?

kapas cotton (ball)

kapri snowpeas

karang coral

karcis ticket

karena because

kartu card

kasar coarse

kasih to give; love

kasur mattress

kata word; say; *berkata* to say

kaus T-shirt; shirt

kaus kaki socks

kawan friend

kawat wire

kawin married; marry;
  perkawinan wedding; marriage

kaya rich

kayu wood

ke to, towards

kebangsaan nationality

kebersihan hygiene, cleanliness

kebetulan accidentally, by chance

kebiasaan habit, custom

kebudayaan culture

kebun garden

kebun binatang zoo

kebun raya botanical gardens

kécap (manis) (sweet) soy sauce

kecapékan tired, fatigue

kecelakaan accident

kecil small

kecuali except

kecut sour

kedua second

kegiatan activity

kejam harsh, cruel

kejar, mengejar to chase

kéju cheese

kejut, terkejut surprised, startled

kelambu mosquito net

kelamin sex, gender

kelapa coconut

kelénténg, klénténg Chinese
  temple

keliling (to go) around

keluar go out, exit

keluarkan, mengeluarkan to
  spend, put out

keluarga family

keluhan complaint

kemarau dry season

kemarin yesterday

kembali return; you're welcome

kembalian change (from a
  purchase)

kembang flower; *berkembang*
  to blossom, develop

kemudian then, afterwards

kena touch, hit, contact, suffer;
  mengenai about, concerning

kenal, mengenal to know,
  recognize, be acquainted;
  kenalan acquaintance

kenangan memories

kenapa? why?; pardon?

kencing urinate

kental thick (of liquids)

kentang potato

kentut fart

kenyang full, having eaten
  enough

kepada to, toward (a person)

kepala head

kepercayaan belief, faith

kepiting crab
keponakan niece or nephew
keputusan decision
kera monkey
keramat sacred
keranjang basket
keras hard
keraton, kraton Javanese palace
kerbau water buffalo
keréta api train
krétek clove cigarette
kering dry
keringat sweat
kerja, bekerja to work
kertas paper
kesal annoyed, angry
kesan impression
kesempatan opportunity, chance
ketat strict
ketawa laugh
ketemu to find, meet
keterangan information
ketiga third
ketinggalan left behind, forgotten
ketok, ketuk knock
khabar, kabar news
khusus special
kilat lightning; express
kini nowadays, presently
kipas fan
kipas angin electric fan
kira, mengira to guess, suppose
kira-kira approximately
kiri left
kirim, mengirim to send

kita we (including person addressed)
klénténg, kelénténg Chinese temple
kol cabbage
kolam pool
kolam renang swimming pool
kontan cash
kopi coffee
kopér suitcase
koran newspaper
korban victim
kosong empty
kota city, town, downtown
kotak box
kotor dirty
kraton, keraton Javanese palace
kuah broth
kuasa power, authority
kuat strong, energetic
kuatir afraid, to worry
kuburan cemetery
kucing cat
kuda horse
kué cake, cookie, pastry
kuku fingernail
kukus steam, steamed
kulit skin, leather
kumis moustache
kumpul gather
kunang-kunang firefly
kunci key; lock
kuning yellow
kunjungan a visit; *berkunjung, mengunjungi* to visit

kuno ancient
kupas, mengupas to peel
kupu-kupu butterfly
kura-kura turtle
kurang less
kurangi, mengurangi to reduce
kurs exchange rate
kursi chair
kurus thin

L

laci drawer
lada pepper
lagi more
lagu song
lahir born
lahirkan, melahirkan to give
  birth
lain different; *selain* apart from
laki-laki male
laku, berlaku sold, valid
lakukan, melakukan to do
lalu past; then
lama old (of things); a long
  time; slow
lambat slow
lampu light, lamp
lancar smooth, proficient, fluent
langganan customer
langit sky
langka rare, scarce
langkah step
langsung directly, non-stop
lantai floor
lapang spacious

lapangan field
lapar hungry
lapis layer
lapor, melapor to report
laporan report
larang, melarang to forbid;
  dilarang forbidden
lari run, escape
latihan practice
laut sea
lawan oppose; opponent
layan, melayani to serve (food
  etc); *layanan* service
layar, berlayar screen; sail; to sail
lébar wide, width
lebih more
lebih banyak more of (a quantity)
léhér neck
lemah weak
lembut soft, gentle
lengan arm
lengkap complete
lepas release, let go
letak place, location; *terletak*
  located
léwat go through, via, past
lidah tongue
lihat, melihat to see, look;
  memperlihat to show
lilin candle, wax
lima five
limau lime
lindungi, melindungi to protect
lipat, melipat to fold
listrik electricity
lokét ticket window, counter

lombok chili pepper
lompat, melompat to jump
losmén homestay, small hotel
luar outside
luar negeri overseas
luas broad, spacious
lubang, lobang hole
lucu funny, amusing
luka injury, injured
lukis, melukis to paint
lukisan painting
lumayan okay, not bad
lunas paid
lupa forget; forgotten
lupakan, melupakan to forget about
lurus straight
lusa the day after tomorrow

M

ma'af! sorry!
mabuk drunk
macam kind
macan tiger
madu honey
mahal expensive
main play; *bermain* to play; *mainan* toy
majalah magazine
maju advance, move forward
makam grave
makan eat; *makanan* food
maksud meaning, intention
malam night
malas lazy

malu ashamed, shy, embarrassed
mampir stop by, visit
mana where
mandi bathe
mangkok bowl
manis sweet
marah angry
mari please, go ahead, let's
masa period; *masa depan* future
masak to cook
masakan cooking, cuisine
masalah problem
masih still
masuk come in, enter
masukkan, memasukkan to put inside
mata eye
matahari sun
matang well-cooked, ripe, well-done
mati die, dead
mau want; going to
me- active verb prefix
méja table
melahirkan to give birth
melakukan to do
melalui by way of, via
melapor to report
melarang to forbid, ban
melayani to serve (food etc)
melihat to look, see
melindungi to protect
melipat to fold
melompat to jump

melukis to paint
melupakan to forget about
memahat to sculpt
memakai to use, wear
memaksa to force
memang indeed
memanggil to call, summon
memasang to switch on, assemble
memBéréskan to solve, arrange
memberi to give
membersihkan to clean
membetulkan to correct, fix
membiarkan to let
memborong to buy up
membosankan boring
membuang to throw out
membuat to make
membuka to open
membunuh to kill, murder
memegang to hold, grasp
memeriksa to examine, inspect
memesan to order (food etc)
memijat to massage
memilih to choose
memiliki to own, possess
meminjam to borrow
memotong to cut
memperbaiki to fix, improve
memperbesar to enlarge
memperlihat to show
memperpanjang to extend, lengthen
mempunyai to have, own
memukul to hit
memutuskan to decide

menanam to plant
menang to win
menangis to cry
menantu son/daughter-in-law
menara tower
menarik interesting; to pull
mencapai to reach, attain
mencari to look for
menceritakan to tell (something)
mencerminkan to reflect
mencétak to print
mencintai to love
mencium to kiss, smell
mencoba to try (on)
mencuci to wash
mencuri to steal
mendampingi to accompany
mendapat to get, reach, receive
mendarat to land
mendekati to approach
mendengar to hear; *mendengarkan* to listen to
mendirikan to build, establish
mendorong to push
mendung cloudy
mengadu to complain
mengajar to teach
mengalahkan to defeat
mengambil to take
mengangkat to lift up
mengantar to guide, lead
mengantuk sleepy
mengejar to chase
mengenai about, concerning

mengeluarkan to spend, put out

mengenal to know, be acquainted with

mengerti to understand

menggambarkan to draw, describe

mengganggu to annoy, disturb

menggantikan to change, replace

menggunakan to (make) use (of)

menghabiskan to finish (off)

menghadapi to face, confront

menghadiri to attend

menghambat to hinder

menghancurkan to destroy

menghasilkan to produce

menghilangkan to get rid of

menghubungi to contact

mengijinkan to permit

mengikuti to follow or go along, accompany

menginap to stay overnight

mengingatkan to remind

mengisap to inhale, suck

mengisi to fill

mengirim to send

mengizinkan to permit

mengupas to peel

mengurangi to reduce

menikah to marry; married

meninggal to pass away

meninggalkan to leave behind

menjadi to become, happen

menjaga to guard

menjahit to sew

menjamin to guarantee, assure

menjawab to answer, reply

menjelaskan to explain, clarify

menjemput to pick someone up

menjual to sell

mentah raw, uncooked, rare

mentéga butter

menurut according to

menyadari to realize, be conscious of

menyambungkan to connect

menyambut to welcome, receive (of persons)

menyelidiki to investigate, research

menyemprot to spray

menyentuh to touch

menyéwa to rent; *menyéwakan* to rent out

menyikat to brush

menyimpan to keep, store

menyukai to like

menyuruh to instruct, command

menyusul to follow behind

mérah red

merasakan to feel

merayakan to celebrate

merdéka free

meréka they, them

merépotkan to trouble

merica pepper

merokok to smoke

mertua father/mother-in-law

mesjid mosque

mesti necessary, should

méwah lavish, expensive

mie noodles

milik own; possession;
  memiliki to own, possess

milyar billion

mimpi dream

Minggu Sunday

minggu week

minta ask for, request

minum to drink

minuman drink

minyak oil

miskin poor

mobil car, automobile

mogok break down (of machines)

mohon request

motor motorcycle

muat load, carry, fit inside

muda young, unripe

mudah easy

muka face, across; *permukaan*
  surface

mulai start, begin

mulut mouth

muncul appear

mundur go back, reverse

mungkin maybe, perhaps

muntah vomit

murah cheap

musim season

musuh enemy

N

naik ride, go up, climb

nakal naughty

nama name

nanas pineapple

nanti later

nanti malam tonight

nanti soré this afternoon/
  evening

nasi rice; *nasi goréng* fried rice

negara country, nation

nékat determined

nénék grandmother

ngantuk, mengantuk sleepy

nginap, menginap to stay
  overnight; *penginapan* small
  hotel, accommodation

ngomong say, speak

ngomong-ngomong by the way

nikah, menikah marry, married

nilai level

nomor number

nol zero

nona Miss

nyala lit, burning (flame), on
  (of lights)

nyamuk mosquito

nyanyi, bernyanyi to sing

nyawa life

nyonya madam

O

obat medicine

obral a sale (at reduced prices)

oléh by

oléh-oléh souvenirs

om uncle

ombak wave, surf

omong, ngomong speak
omong kosong nonsense
ongkos cost, expense
orang personorang tua parents

p

pabrik factory
pacar boyfriend or girlfriend
pada on
padang field, square
padi rice plant
pagi morning
paha thigh
pahat, memahat to sculpt
pahit bitter
pajak tax
pakai, memakai to use, wear; *pakaian* clothing
pakét parcel
paksa, memaksa to force
paku nail
paling the most
paling-paling at the most
paman uncle
panas hot (temperature)
pandai smart
pandangan view, panorama
panggang roasted; *memanggang* to roast
panggil, memanggil to call, summon
pangkat rank
panjang long, length; *memperpanjang* to extend, lengthen; *perpanjangan* extension

pantai beach
parah bad, serious (of illness, problems, etc.)
pasang, memasang to assemble, switch on
pasar a market
pasir sand
pasti sure, certain
patah broken (of bones, long objects)
patung statue
payung umbrella
pecah shattered
pedagang trader, seller
pedas hot (spicy)
pegang, memegang to hold, grasp
pejabat government official
pekerjaan job, occupation
pelan slow; *pelan-pelan* slowly
pelaut sailor
pelayan servant
pelayanan service
pemandangan panorama, view
pembunuhan murder, killing
pemerintah government
pemimpin leader
pencuri thief; *pencurian* theft
pendaftaran registration
péndék short
pendéta (Protestant) priest
peneliti researcher; *penelitian* research
pengaduan complaint
pengaruh influence
penginapan small hotel, accommodation

peninggalan remains
penjara jail
penjelasan clarification
penting important
penuh full
penumpang passenger
perahu boat
pérak silver
peran role
perang war
perangko stamp
perayaan celebration
perbédaan difference
perbaikan repairs
perbesar, memperbesar to enlarge
percakapan conversation
percaya believe, trust;
kepercayaan belief, faith
perempuan woman
perempatan crossroads
pergi to go, leave
perhentian (transportation) stop
periksa, memeriksa to examine, inspect
perintah command;
pemerintah government
perjanjian agreement
perkawinan wedding, marriage
perkembangan development
perlihatkan, memperlihatkan to show
perlu need
permén candy
permisi! excuse me!
permukaan surface

pernah already, ever, once
perpanjangan extension
persén percentage
persimpangan intersection
pertama first;
pertama-tama first of all
pertanyaan question
pertunjukan show, performance
perut stomach, belly
pesan order; *memesan* to order (food etc)
pesawat airplane; telephone extension, instrument
pésta party
peta map
peti crate
pijat, memijat massage
pikir, berpikir to think
pikiran thoughts
pilek a cold
pilih, memilih to choose, select
pilihan choice
pindah move (position)
pinjam, meminjam to borrow
pintar smart
pintu door
pipi cheek
piring plate
pisah separate
pisang banana
pisau knife
pohon tree
pompa pump
pompa bénsin gas station
pondok hut, shack

potong, memotong to cut;
  potongan cut, slice
pria man
pribadi private
puas satisfied
pukul, memukul to hit
pulang go back/home
pulau island; *kepulauan*
  archipelago
puluh tens; *puluhan* dozens
puncak peak, summit
punya, mempunyai to have, own
pura Balinese (Hindu) temple
puri Balinese palace
pusat center
pusing dizzy
putar to do a U-turn
putih white
putus break off
putuskan, memutuskan to decide

R

Rabu Wednesday
racun poison
ragu-ragu doubt, doubtful
rahasia secret
raja king
rajin hardworking, industrious
rakyat people
ramah friendly, open
ramai busy, noisy
rambut hair
rantai chain
rapat a meeting
rapi orderly, neat

rasa feeling, taste;
  merasakan to feel
rata even, level
ratu queen
ratus hundred; *ratusan* hundreds
raya large, great
rayakan, merayakan to
  celebrate (a holiday); *perayaan*
  celebration
rebus boiled
rebut fight about, over
regu team
rekan colleague, workmate
rékening bill
remaja youth
rempah-rempah spices
renang, berenang to swim
rencana a plan;
  berencana to plan, planned
rendah low
répot go to trouble, troublesome
répotkan, merépotkan to trouble
resép prescription; recipe
resmi official
retak crack, cracked
ribu thousand; *ribuan* thousands
ringan light (not heavy)
ringkas concise
roda wheel
rok dress
rokok cigarette; *merokok* to
  smoke
roti bread
ruang, ruangan room, hall,
  space
rugi lose money, make a loss

rukun harmonious

rumah house, home; *rumah sakit* hospital

rumit complicated

rumput grass

rupa appearance; *rupanya* it seems

rusa deer

rusak broken

S

saat moment, instant

sabar patient

Sabtu Saturday

sabuk belt; *sabuk pengaman* seatbelt

sabun soap

sadar, menyadari to be conscious of, realize

sahabat friend

saja only

sakit sick; painful

saksi witness

sakti magic power

saku pocket

salah wrong, false

salam greetings

saling mutually

salju snow

sama same; with, using

sama-sama you're welcome

sambal chili sauce

sambil while

sambung, menyambungkan to connect

sambungan connection

sambut, menyambut to receive, welcome (of persons)

sampah garbage

sampai arrive, reach; until

samping side

sana there

sangat very, extremely

sanggup capable, able

santai relaxed

sapi beef, cow

sapu broom

sarang nest

saring filter

sarung sarong, wrap-around cloth

sastra literature

saté barbecued meat on skewers

satu one

saudara sibling; relative, family member

sawah rice paddy

saya I, me

sayang love; a shame

sayap wing

sayur, sayuran vegetables

se- prefix meaning one, the same as

sebab cause, because

sebelah next to

sebelas eleven

sebelum before

sebentar in a moment

seberang across from

sedang in the middle of

sedap delicious

sederhana modest, simple

sedia available

sedih sad

sedikit little, not much

segala all sorts of

segar fresh

segera soon

segi angle, side

séhat healthy

seimbang equal

sejak since

sejarah history

sejuk cool

sekali very; once, one time

sekarang now

sekitar around, about

sekolah school

sékretaris secretary

selain apart from

selamat congratulations, safe

Selasa Tuesday

selat straits

selatan south

selai jam

seléndang shoulder cloth for holding things, sash

selesai to finish

selidiki, menyelidiki to investigate, research

selimut blanket

seluruh entire, whole

semangat spirit

semangka watermelon

sembahyang to pray

sembilan nine

sembuh cured, recovered

sembunyi hide; hidden

sementara temporarily

sempat have an opportunity to; *kesempatan* opportunity

sempit narrow

semprot, menyemprot to spray

sempurna perfect, flawless

semua all

senang like, be pleased

sendiri self, oneself, alone

sendirian by oneself, all alone

séndok spoon

seni art

seniman artist

Senin, Senén Monday

senja dusk

senjata weapon

sentuh, menyentuh to touch

senyum, tersenyum to smile

sepatu shoes

sepéda bicycle

seperempat one quarter

seperti like, as

sepertiga one third

sepi quiet, deserted

sepréi bedsheet

sepuluh ten

serba all sorts

sering often

serta, beserta with

sesuai dengan adapted to, suited to

sesuaikan, menyesuaikan to adapt to

sesudah after

setasium railway station

setelah after

setengah half

setia loyal

séwa, menyéwa to rent

séwakan, menyéwakan to rent out

sia-sia to no avail

siang middle of the day

siap, bersiap ready

siapkan, mempersiapkan to make ready

siapa? who?

siaran a broadcast, program

sibuk busy

sifat characteristic

sikap attitude

sikat a brush; *menyikat* to brush

silakan, silahkan please

simpan, menyimpan to keep, store

simpang intersection; *menyimpang* to diverge from

sinar ray

singkat concise

sini here

sisa leftover, remainder

sisi side, flank

sisir comb; *menyisir* to comb

situ over there

soal matter, problem

sop clear soup

sopir, supir driver

soré late afternoon (3 pm to dusk)

soto Indonesian meat soup

suami husband

suara voice

suasana atmosphere

suatu a certain

subur fertile

sudah already

suhu temperature

suka, menyukai to like

sukar difficult

suku tribe, people

suling flute

sulit difficult

sumpit chopsticks

sumur a well

sungai river

sungguh really, truly

suntik inject, vaccinate; *suntikan* needle; injection

supaya so that

surat letter, document

surat kabar newspaper

suruh, menyuruh to instruct, command

susah difficult

susu milk

susul, menyusul to follow

sutera silk

syarat precondition, condition

T

tadi just now

tadi malam last night

tafsir, menafsir to guess, estimate

tagih, menagih to collect payment

tahan hold back, restrain, bear, survive

tahu know

tahu soybean curd

tahun year

tajam sharp

takut scared, afraid

tali rope, string

taman garden

tamat end, finish

tambah add, increase

tamu guest

tanah earth, land

tanam, menanam to plant, invest

tanaman plant

tanda sign, indication

tanda tangan signature

tangan hand, forearm

tangga stair, step

tanggal date (of the month)

tanggap, menanggapi to react, respond

tanggapan reaction, response

tanggung jawab responsibility

tangis, menangis to cry

tangkap, menangkap to catch, capture

tanpa without

tantangan challenge

tante aunt

tanya, bertanya to ask

tari, menari to dance

tarian dance

tarik to pull

tarip tariff, fare

taruh, menaruh to put, place

tas bag, purse

tawar, menawar to make an offer, bargain

tebal thick

tebu sugarcane

tegang tense

tegur warn, tell off

teguran warning

téh tea

tekan to press

tekanan pressure

telaga lake, pond

telanjang naked

telinga ear

teliti careful, meticulous

teluk bay

telur egg

teman friend

témbok wall

tembus, menembus to pierce, penetrate, soak through

tempat place

tempat tidur bed

témpé fermented soybean cake

témpél, menémpél to stick

temu, bertemu, menemui to meet

tenaga power

tenang calm

tengah middle

tenggara southeast

tenggelam submerged, drowned

téngok, menéngok to see, visit

tentang concerning, about

tentara army

tentu certain, certainly

tentukan, menentukan to fix a
time, to establish

tenun, menenun to weave

tenun, tenunan weavings

tepat exact, exactly

tepi edge, fringe

tepung flour

terakhir last

terang light, clear, bright

terbalik reversed, backwards

terbang to fly

terbit, menerbitkan published;
to publish

tercatat registered (post)

tergantung it depends, to
depend on

terhadap regarding, towards,
against

teriak shout

terima receive

terima kasih thank you

terjadi happen

terjun fall, tumble down

terkejut surprised

terlalu too (excessive)

terlambat late

terminal bus station

térong eggplant, aubergine

tersembunyi hidden

tertawa to laugh

terus straight ahead

teruskan, meneruskan to
continue

tetap fixed, permanent

tetapi but

tiang post, column

tiap every

tiba arrive

tiba-tiba suddenly

tidak no, not

tidak mungkin impossible

tidak usah not necessary

tidur sleep

tiga three

tiga belas thirteen

tikar mat

tikus mouse, rat

timbang weigh

timbangan scales

timbangkan, mempertimbangkan
to consider

timbul appear, emerge from

timun cucumber

timur east

tindak, bertindak to act

tinggal live, reside, stay

tinggalkan, meninggalkan to
leave behind

tinggi tall, high

tingkat level, story of a building

tinjau, meninjau to survey

tipis thin (not thick)

tipu, menipu to deceive, cheat,
trick

tiram oyster

titip deposit, leave with
someone

toko store, shop

tolak, menolak to refuse

tolong, menolong to help, assist

tomat tomato

tonjol, menonjol to stick out

tonton, menonton to watch, observe

topéng mask

topi hat

tua old

tuak palm wine

tuan sir

tuang, menuangkan to pour

tubuh body

tugas job, duties

tugu monument

tuju, menuju towards

tujuan destination, goal

tujuh seven

tukang craftsman, tradesman

tukar, menukar to exchange

tulang bone

tulis, menulis to write

tumbuh, bertumbuh to grow (larger, up); *tumbuhan* growth, plant

tumbuk to pound

tunai in cash

tunda, ditunda to postpone; be postponed

tunggal single, sole

tunggu, menunggu to wait, wait for

tunjuk point out, show

tuntut, menuntut to demand

turun go down, get off

turut to obey

tusuk skewer

tutup, menutup to close, cover

U

uang money

uap steam

ubah, berubah to change

ucapkan, menucapkan to express, say

udang shrimp, prawn

udara air

uji to test

uji coba try out

ujian test

ujung tip, point, spit (of land)

ukir, mengukir to carve

ukiran carving

ukur, mengukur to measure

ukuran measurement, size

ulang, mengulangi to repeat

ular snake

umpama example

umpamanya for example

umum general, public

umumnya generally

umur age

undang, mengundang to invite

undangan invitation

untuk for, to

untung profit, luck, benefit

upacara ceremony

urat sinews, tendons

urus arrange

urut be in sequence

usaha efforts, activities

usir, mengusir to chase away, out

utama main, chief

utang debt

utara north

utuh whole, complete

W

waktu when; time

wanita lady

warga negara citizen

warna color

warta berita news; *wartawan* journalist

warung roadside stall

watak character, personality

wayang puppet or dance performance

wayang kulit shadow puppet play

wayang orang traditional Javanese theater

wisma guesthouse

wortel carrot

Y

ya yes

yakin to believe

yang (the one) who, that, which